Kurtis - Kraft Midget

A Genealogy of Speed

An Illustrated History by Bill Montgomery

Kurtis - Kraft Midget A Genealogy of Speed
by Bill Montgomery

Published by: Witness Productions
Box 34, Church St.
Marshall, IN 47859
765-597-2487

ISBN 1-891390-02-3

Front Cover: The famous Ashley Wright Kurtis Kraft Midget
            Photo by Jim Chini.

Printed in the U.S.A.

Hudson M. Meyer 1942 - 1997

This book is dedicated to his memory.

CONTENTS

PREFACE

This book contains all of the information that I have collected in twenty years of research on the midget race cars produced by Frank Kurtis.

Since the publication of my two articles in "Auto Racing Memories and Memorabilia" in 1986, many people - mistakenly, assumed that the records I had compiled on K.K. midgets contained the histories of the majority of the cars produced by the company.

The information included in these pages represents the fragmented histories of approximately one half of the midgets Frank Kurtis produced, (271 uprights and 10 roadsters).

The loss of the records of Kurtis midget production was a blow to historians researching this durable little racer, however procuring the names of the original buyers would not resolve the question of subsequent ownership. This book tries, in some small way, to resolve the question, with the help of written and oral histories that I have accumulated in the past two decades.

Researching the histories of K.K. midgets has been costly, and time consuming. I would be less than truthful if I did not add that at times I tired of the project and doubted that it would ever be completed.

Now that I have come to the end of my journey, I hope that this volume will aid those people seeking information about Kurtis - Kraft midgets. If this work inspires, and stimulates others to commit their memories to the written page before this important page of Americana is lost forever, so much the better.

ACKNOWLEDGMENTS

Every writer who puts together a work of this kind needs the help and inspiration of many people. The information in these pages has been pieced together from racing records, periodicals, photos and human resources. I know the reader usually skips past this part to get to, "the good stuff". Please resist the temptation and take a few moments to peruse the names of the people that helped make this book a reality - people like; Frank Kurtis, George Shilala, Arlen Kurtis, Johnny Pawl, Hudson Meyer, Jack Marsden, Jack Fox, Jim Montgomery, Mike Amato, Jim Chini, Ronnie Allyn, Bruce Craig, Leroy Byers, Dal Ewing, Stan Lobitz, Tom Motter, Bob Bamford, Rick Wold, Marty Himes, Fred Johns, Gordon White, Tommy Morrow, Ollie Johnson, Al Hall, Joe De Maio, Bill Hill, Freddie Chaparro, Barry Knowlton, Danny Frye, Frank Burany, Emil Andres, Grant Marceau, Derek Lewin, Bert and Arnold Krause, Bill Krech, Jim Barclay, Ken Hickey, Phil Walters (Ted Tappett), Georgie Rice, Sam Traylor, Spike Gillespie, Jim Witzler, Jim Aashe, Tom Palmer and other too numerous to mention.

The impetus to complete this book, is in response to the death of my cousin, Hudson Meyer on February 16, 1997; and the realization that it was time to put my affairs in order, so to speak.

For years, Hudson and I talked about producing, the Kurtis - Kraft Midget Book. We quibbled over format, documentation and the inevitable gaps in continuity that accrue to such an endeavor. Fearing reproaches - a book never materialized.

It is obvious, at this late date that the Kurtis - Kraft mystery will never be completely unraveled and further delay is unwarranted.

For inspiration and constructive help I wish to extend special thanks to my loving wife, Patricia, and my stepson, Scott Clark, who constantly urged me to finish this work.

I hope this volume will be helpful to future generations who rediscover the remarkable contribution of Frank Kurtis and his profound legacy to American auto racing.

Lastly, this historical document would not have the stature it does without the magnificent photos supplied by Jim Chini and Jim Montgomery. You will find their photos identified throughout the book by the words: *J.C. Collection and J.M. Collection.*

Kurtis - Kraft Midget

A Genealogy of Speed

An Illustrated History by Bill Montgomery

Witness Productions

P.O. Box 34, Marshall, IN 47859

―― Dream Age ――

Los Angeles, unlike New York and Chicago, was a city built on dreams. A product of the motion picture industry and flamboyant land developers.

In the 1920s and 1930s the wealthy and affluent enjoyed the good life in sunny Southern California. That image changed when the Second World War brought the defense industry to Los Angeles.

In 1946 the city of Los Angeles was a sprawling megalopolis, encircled by a cluster of bedroom communities. The booming economy in blue collar factory and construction jobs caused a housing scarcity. Houses sold for $5,000.00 and the Angelinos complained that you couldn't buy a meal at a restaurant for less than 65 cents.

After twelve years of economic depression and four years of bloody war a great burden had been lifted. There was a feeling that anyone with vision, capital and guts could do just about anything. The people of this great country were ready to cut loose and have a party!

It was in this euphoric atmosphere that Frank Kurtis, the 37 year old son of Croatian immigrants completed the prototype of the Kurtis - Kraft midget race car, a race car whose achievements would become legendary in the history of American oval track racing.

By early 1945 Kurtis could see the war was winding down. He developed his prototype midget and by the end of 1945 he was ready to start booking orders.

He tried to interest the most able men in racing. Men like Rex Mays, Perry Grimm, Johnny Balch, Gib Lilly and Roy Russing.

When the first Kurtis - Kraft midgets appeared at the legendary Gilmore Stadium on Beverly Boulevard and the Los Angeles Coliseum they were an instant sensation.

Frank Kurtis proudly poses next to the first K.K. Midget with owner Roy Russing.

Writers and Photographers filled magazines and newspapers with stories about the sleek new racers with pictures of begrimed drivers kissing beautiful starlets. Luminaries from the entertainment industry like Clark Gable, Carole Landis, Mel Torme, Keenan Wynn, Eddie "Rochester" Anderson and Donald O'Connor were drawn to the new entertainment phenomenon.

Actor Donald O'Connor and Gib Lilly bench race.

Tony Aglar forming an aluminum panel.

Franks original shop, located at 525 West Colorado Blvd. in Glendale, was too small to adequately handle the flood of orders for his new midget so he moved to a larger facility at 4625 Alger Street in Burbank.

Frank needed a competent crew and a foreman with sound organizational skills to turn his dreams into a tangible product.

According to former employee, Everett Duncan, the first shop foreman was "Mush" Johnson. George Shilala was the second foreman. This might account for the confusion about the numbering of the first few chassis. We will get back to this subject in much greater depth, later.

Bill Kurtis, Frank's brother, was the office manager. Other front office men, responsible for layout and drafting, were Avard, Joe and George Ward.

The crew, responsible for the actual manufacture of Kurtis - Kraft midgets, consisted of: Power hammer operator, Tony Aglar, Welders: Harry Pitford, "Mush" Johnson, Harry Miller, Bob Lee and from time to time, 1950 Indy winner, Johnnie Parsons.

Assembly was performed by Carl Blackmar, Avard Ward, Ernie Wheatley and Don Allen.

In-house machine work and fabrication was accomplished by Bill Coffin, Don Allen, Tom Barnes, Sylvester Fredricks and Carl Newhall.

Exhaust headers were built by Bernie Rich and Rudy Capranica. Rudy also did the in-house louver work.

Frank Kurtis employed some of the finest metalmen in the country to shape the aluminum into a finished product. His crew included: Quinn Epperly, Wayne Ewing, Emil Deidt and Harry Stephens.

Hoods, belly pans and radiator shells were built by Ed Justice. Ernie Wheatley built carburetor panels. Ward Miller, Frank's brother-in-law, worked as a trimmer. Indy veteran, Chet Miller, worked as an upholsterer and final fit and finish was left to Tony Colnar.

Some of the work was accomplished by outside contractors. Eddie Vogel, from Riverside, did some of the machine work. Bob Stelling in Burbank built V8-60 headers and in-and-out gear boxes. Lauren Bennett and Ernie Casale provided quick change rear ends and Norden and Evans supplied the steering boxes. From Roy Richter, of Bell Auto Parts, came the steering wheels and hand pumps.

The inevitable crash work was handled by Everett Duncan, Lawrence "Zeke" Justice and the fiery tempered, Louis Salzgaber.

The Kurtis - Kraft production line in 1947.

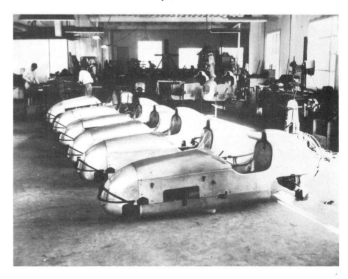

Everett Duncan described the basic assembly procedure of a K.K. midget.

First, the frames were welded and the steering box was installed, after that the firewall was fitted into place. The next operation was the installation of the instrument panel which was attached to the cowl hoop with sheet metal screws. The side panel and radiator shell were installed and the car was rotated upside down so the belly pans could be fitted in place. If heel wells were desired they were hammered out into a kirksite die by "Zeke" Justice. It took two men to bend the belly pans over a 5" steel pipe. If louvers were ordered by the customer, Art Ingalls punched them. Next the various panels were drilled for dzus buttons. The car was turned back over into an upright position. The tail was trimmed and rolled, and the fueling hole was cut in the headrest. The last operation was installation of the hood which required trimming and shrinking with a hammer and dolly.

A very early 1946 K.K. midget being fabricated.

Chapter One

Controversy and Confusion

"The Mighty Midgets" by Jack Fox, " The Kurtis - Kraft Story" by Ed Hitze and "When The Coliseum Roared" by T.C. Redd were three important books about midget racing in the post war period. All of these volumes stated that a total of 1100 midgets were built by Kurtis - Kraft, 550 complete cars and 550 kit cars.

In twenty years of research, the highest legitimate chassis number I have come across is 367. The highest numbered kit car is X 152. The sum of those two numbers is 519, far short of the oft quoted 1100 figure, closer to a total of 550!

I cannot say that the exercise that I used to arrive at the sum of 519 is infallible, however it would seem reasonable to assume that in a random sampling of hundreds of correspondents all over the country I might have come up with a few numbers in the 400 series or 500 series if those number series existed.

To add fuel to the fire, the dash tag carrying the number 367 indicates the car was produced in November of 1952, two months before Kurtis sold the midget division to Johnny Pawl in 1953! It is important to note that Pawl did not continue the practice of chassis numbering.

A little sleuthing shows how sharp the downturn in K.K. production was, when the midget boom turned to a bust, and the stock cars came on strong.

According to my records Kurtis built no more than 26 midgets in 1949. Between 1950 and 1951 only 2 cars were built and 2 cars were built in 1952!

If Kurtis were to have produced 550 complete cars he would have had to have produced 182 complete cars in two months - an impossibility!

In an effort to be as impartial as possible I contacted George Shilala, the Kurtis shop foreman who initiated the numbering system. I asked George his best recollection of the total number of midgets produced by Kurtis - Kraft, without hesitation George said he believed the total number of *cars* produced by Kurtis was 688. I have discussed this with Arlen Kurtis who helped me with some of the numbers. Arlen said he believed his father produced 128 champ cars, 17 sports cars and 10 midget roadsters. My numbers indicated 367 midgets complete and 172 midget kit cars. Shilala thought 4 or 5 sprint cars were built. That would make a grand total of 699 cars. This number is only 11 cars more than the number cited by Shilala - more than a coincidence?

In December of 1998, Grant Marceau, from Rhode Island, contacted me about several K.K. midgets he had purchased. In the course of the conversation, Grant innocently mentioned a letter Frank Kurtis had written to "Speed Age" Magazine in February, 1952 in which he stated that he had only built **550 midget race cars!**

Grant was good enough to send me a photocopy of the page from "Speed Age" containing the letter.

I include the unedited letter, in its entirety.

Frank Kurtis next to an Indy Car chassis in the welding jig.

Editor, Speed Age:

For a considerable length of time I have wanted to write to you and tell you how much I enjoy and look forward to reading Russ Catlin's interesting and authentic articles on automobile racing.

His recent *Midgets Tried Again-and Won* has in one paragraph a statement by Harry Stephens which is without justification to Kurtis - Kraft, as he, too, owned a Kurtis - Kraft midget, and was unable to outdo some of the "production mechanics," as he called them. He, in turn, sold the car to Mike Caruso; the same car won 58 races in one season with Bill Schindler driving.

We have been condemned on numerous occasions for producing as many midgets as we did. Our original plans were to produce 30 cars only, but when Solar Aircraft and others went into production, we felt that our produce was of a safer and better construction that we continued the manufacture and sold over **550** units. I might add that a great deal of my time was spent in trying to discourage many potential customers from buying cars because it was evident that we were having too many races and the time would eventually come when people would tire of a repetition of practically the same type of program.

On the other hand, it might be reasonable to assume that we, to some extent, could have been partially responsible for the limited success of midget auto racing due to the appearance and performance of our equipment.

It has never been noted that the success of cars like our old car, now owned by Jim Robbins, Belanger's No. 99, the Novis, and many others, were developed and built by our firm, plus the fact that the majority of the racing cars have parts and equipment of our manufacture. Therefore if credit to the above facts are not given, why do remarks of criticism always come to print?

We are now in the last stages of completion on the new Cummins Diesel race car and will have the car at the Wichita University for extensive wind tunnel tests. I am sure you will find many features of interest in this particular car."

Frank Kurtis,
Los Angeles, Calif.

Chassis Markings and Dash Tags

Kurtis - Kraft sold complete, ready to run, race cars and cars referred to as "kit cars." A kit car, as the name implies, was a car sold minus components, such as, an engine, rear end or steering box that the new owner preferred to add himself.

The kit cars were marked with an X before the serial number while complete cars were *usually* marked with only the serial number.

The car was also fitted with an aluminum dash plaque. A letter prefix designated the engine type with a double digit number after the serial number. This designated the year of manufacture. A dash tag with an alpha numeric designation like F-30-46 would indicated the car was powered by a Ford V8-60 engine. It would have been the thirtieth car produced by the company and it would have been built in 1946. If the car possessed an O before the serial number it would have been powered by an Offenhauser engine.

Author and historian, Gordon White has researched the evolution of the dash tag and is currently reproducing a facsimile of the original for restorers who have purchased a car that has had the tag removed. Gordon says the K.K. dash plaque before 1948 was red and the dash tag after 1948 was black.

An "X" Theory

Gordon White was curious about the subject of X prefix chassis. He asked about the X numbered chassis I had come across. I related that I found X prefix chassis in the 70, 80, 90, 100, 110 and 120 series. The earliest X number I found was X 71.

I knew that car was produced in 1947 for Bill Vukovich.

We discussed the coded number Frank used on the Champ cars and we deduced that a similar code may have been used on midgets.

Gordon said perhaps the first digit was the year and the second digit the serial number.

In the case of the Vukovich car it would translate to the first car built in 1947 (7=1947 - 1= Chassis #1).

This hypothesis is interesting. Common sense would dictate that Vuky's car would have been a high priority job for Kurtis who would have viewed it as a triumph for Vukovich to abandon his potent pre-war rail Drake for a K.K. chassis.

Another puzzle that is yet to be solved, is the lack of any X chassis in the 10, 20, 30, 40, 50 and 60 number sequence.

Bill Vukovich in chassis X 71 - The first "kit" car or the seventy first "kit" car?

I.D. Number Location

The chassis numbers stamped in the frame can usually be found on the upper surface of the main frame member between the two small pieces of tubing that form the cowl hoop on both the right and left side of the chassis. An identical set of numbers can sometimes be found on the top of the rear crossmember on the right hand side.

The fabricator who was responsible for stamping the chassis numbers used steel stamping dies and simply gave the die a sharp rap with a ball-peen hammer. As a result of this imprecise method, the numbers sometimes run up and down hill, and may be quite faint, or in some cases only partially complete. A #8 or a #9 can be mistaken for a #3. Over time the numbers have become increasingly difficult to read, due to grinding, sand and bead blasting.

Identical Numbers

This question can be partially, but not completely answered. Some of the duplications might be attributed to carelessness or confusion on the part of the fabricator who may have assumed that the next number in the sequence was, in fact the last number that had been used.

After George Shilala left Kurtis - Kraft he built about fifty midget race cars that were virtually identical to the K.K.

He stamped these cars the same way he marked the midgets at Kurtis - Kraft! This complicates an already complicated situation for the collectors who own cars numbered 1-50!

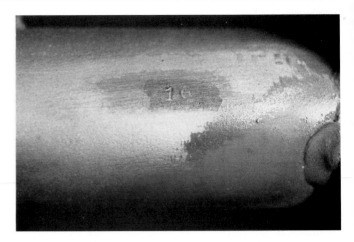

An extreme close-up view of a chassis stamped with the number "16". This car is the famous Kittinger and Redding V8-60.

Shilala's Numbers

I asked George how the number system got started and I was surprised to find that it was his idea! He said he wanted a record of the people who welded a particular car in case any legal action arose as a result of an injury or fatality caused by faulty workmanship. George was ahead of his time! George added that when he began the process Frank told him it was a waste of time because they wouldn't build more than 25 cars. This conversation is borne out in the letter Frank Kurtis wrote to *Speed Age* stating that he only planned to build 30 cars!

Lujie Lesovsky, left and Quinn Epperly work on the Brown Motor Freight Indy car.

First Ten Cars

Shilala was adamant that the first ten cars produced were stamped. He said that they were all in the shop when he started working there and he stamped all of them. He did say that the ten cars may not have been in the exact order in which they were built because he had no knowledge of the actual order in which they were started.

Since it has been reported that two of the earliest cars, Roy Russing's Offy and Bill Krech's Offy, were unnumbered I believe it possible that an indeterminable number of cars were built before George Shilala went to work for Kurtis - Kraft.

Kurtis managed to get out the first few cars, e.g. Russing, Balch, Mays, Krech, Bennett, Edwards and Lilly's out of the shop before the dam broke. At that point he knew he was going to need a competent foreman to straighten out the chaos.

The above scenario fits the account given by long time Kurtis employee, Everett Duncan, (1946-1954). Everett told historian and author Tom Motter in a taped interview, that the first cars were such an immediate success that the prospective owners had to come down to the shop to work on their own cars! Everett named people like Lauren Bennett, Rudy Sumpter and Marv Edwards. It is also interesting to note that in Mr. Duncan's recollections of the original members of the crew George Shilala was not named as the first foreman. He was apparently brought on board after "Mush" Johnson served in that capacity.

Unmarked Chassis

There are some K.K. chassis that do not have a number stamped on the frame. I attribute this to an oversight by the person stamping the car, welding and grinding damage, or a chassis being one of the first 10 to 12 cars built.

I spoke to Barry Knowlton, a very knowledgeable owner of the first K.K. built, (Roy Russing's car). Barry swore there was no number on that chassis. This makes sense in light of the fact the car was a prototype built in late 1945 to sell a concept.

Although many collectors are interested in numbered chassis I felt it necessary to include a section on cars whose histories were known but whose chassis number was unknown.

We may never know the chassis number of some historically important cars but that doesn't seem to be a valid reason to ignore them.

Midwest Connection

Another 50 cars were produced by Johnny Pawl when he bought the midget part of Kurtis - Kraft. In personal communication he told me he didn't mark his chassis.

This brings up an interesting academic question. What constitutes a genuine Kurtis - Kraft midget?

Since Kurtis - Kraft was sold to Johnny Pawl it would seem that a car produced by Pawl would have to be recognized as a K.K., albeit an Indiana K.K. rather than a Glendale or Burbank K.K. I will leave this debate to others.

The Book

Stories have circulated for years about a book that contained all the chassis numbers and the owners of all the cars produced by Frank Kurtis. The story took on mythical proportions. Did such a book exist? It was like the search for the Holy Grail.

I contacted George Shilala who told me there were two such books that contained the names of all the original owners of K.K. midgets!

One book was a loose-leaf shop book and the other was a gray bound 9" by 12" ledger that recorded the names of the fabricators who welded the cars. George went on to say that the loose-leaf recorded the chassis number owner and also included sketches of the cars, noting wheelbase and suspension details so he could build a "sister" car if someone wanted a car just like it.

Barry Knowlton, an owner driver and Kurtis - Kraft employee, told me he used to skim through the pages of the loose-leaf copy of the book during lunch when he worked at the Kurtis shop in 1961.

I am convinced at this time that neither of these books will surface. They may have been lost, stolen or destroyed. Another possibility is that they were callously discarded for reasons that are unclear. For whatever reason these most significant records are probably gone forever.

—— Chapter Two ——

The First K.K. Midget

The first car built was obviously Roy Russing's teal #75 Offy.

For years it was said that Russing never drove his car in competition. This is refuted by photos and documents that clearly show that Russing drove the car in competition on two occasions - April 7, 1946 and April 14, 1946 at Stockton, California. After Russing's death on April 21, 1946, at Stockton in the Prickett Offy, his wife ran the car with Gordon Cleveland behind the wheel.

In 1950, Jo Russing sold the car to Gus Linhares. Linhares campaigned the car with a V8-60 engine. Linhares transferred ownership to Norm Innis who also ran the car as a V8-60.

Bob Curtin bought the car from Innis, painted it blue and yellow with a #34. It ran as a V8-60 in U.R.A. Curtin was killed in the car while qualifying at San Bernardino on July 27, 1956.

The car was sold to Brad Isaacson and Woody Bennett. They ran the car as an orange and white #40 V8-60. Isaacson and Bennett parted company with Brad as the owner.

Barry Knowlton, the next owner painted the car pink and white. Jon Ward purchased the car from Knowlton and ran it as a white #91 powered by a V8-60. Jon Ward sold the car back to Knowlton who in turn sold it back to Ward.

Jon Ward sold it to his brother Tom who sold it to Harvey Guttry. Guttry ran the car as a white #99 V8-60.

The car moved to the San Francisco Bay Area when it was bought by Ron Raible. Raible ran the car as a black and red Chevy II.

Raible sold the car to Johnny Soares, Jr. who ran it as a white and blue #08 Chevy II.

The car went back to Southern California to Loren Chiever who was the last man to actively campaign it.

Loren sold the car to Tom Oakley in 1985. Oakley planned to restore the car. Oakley died and his family sold the car to Joe Riker in 1988.

Joe also planned to restore the car. Arlen Kurtis found out that Joe had the car and he bought it in 1995.

So the 50 year sojourn that began in the Frank Kurtis shop ended in the hands of his son.

Above: Likable Dick Atkins in the Ron Raible V8-60.

Above: Photographic proof that Russing drove his own car in competition. Russing at Stockton, California, April 1946.

Below: Bob Curtin in the former Russing car with V8-60 power. Bob was the only driver to lose his life in the car.

Above: The original lines of the Russing Offy are difficult to distinguish in this late incarnation of the car. The owner/driver is Johnny Soares Jr.

Chapter Three

1946 Numbered Chassis

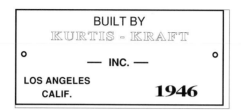

BUILT BY

KURTIS - KRAFT

— INC. —

LOS ANGELES
CALIF.   **1946**

Chapter Three

1946 Numbered Chassis

Chassis 02

While undergoing restoration in Bob Willey's shop Bob discovered the #02 on the frame of the former Gregory Flatow Offy. The car was thought to be an older K.K. Pictures of Gene Hartley in Flatow's "D & D Heet" sponsored #52 reveal quarter elliptical springs; clear evidence of an early chassis.

In later years, Flatow ran the car as a yellow and black #52 Offy with drivers like Jud Larson, Rodger Ward, Roger McCluskey, Jim McElreath and Bill Homeier behind the wheel.

Flatow sold the car to Johnny Tibbens. Little is known about the car while in his ownership.

Tibbens sold the car to Johnny Hobel. Hobel wanted to replicate the red and white #12 V8-60 midget he drove for Al Willey in the late 40s.

Roger McCluskey finesses the Flatow Offy at Allentown, PA. in 1966.

Bob Willey turned the former Flatow car into a replica of his fathers car for Hobel.

Johnny Hobel sold the car to Jim McDonald in Illinois.

Chassis 03 ▶

One of the best documented early Kurtis's was purchased by Lloyd Axel in 1946. The car was a white #5 Offy that won hundreds of races.

Axel sold the car to Eddie Jackson who also ran it as a white #5 Offy.

Vern Shaver bought the car from Jackson but Eddie hankered for the "Old Iron" and bought it back.

Jackson finally sold the car to Milt Goldman. The car still looked very much like the old Axel car, with the addition of cross torsion bars and a cage.

Goldman sold the car to Harry Conklin, the last man to campaign the car competitively.

As of 1983 it was in the possession of Denver R.M.M.R.A. photographer, Leroy Byers.

A youthful Gene Hartley in the "D & D Heet" sponsored, Greg Flatow Offy c. 1947.

Lloyd Axel in his white #5 Offy. The car is now part of the Leroy Byers collection.

The Lloyd Axel car, less body panels, reveals the simple, yet rugged construction of the K.K. chassis

Eddie Jackson kept Lloyd Axel's old car in the winners circle.

Leo Tucker in the Goldman Offy. Leo won the Roy Leslie Memorial race in September of 1974 in the former Axel car, nearly 28 years after its first feature win.

Chassis 04

duplicate

This car was originally out of the Pacific Northwest. Tom Carstens was the first owner of the white and blue #44 V8-60 driven to countless wins by the indomitable Allen Heath. Heath relocated in Southern California and ran the car in U.R.A.'s "Red Circuit" with great success.

Tom Carstens sold the car to Dick Cowan and Cowan sold the car to Dickie Deis.

Deis ran it with three different engines during his ownership. Originally it was powered by a V8-60 then a Volvo and finally an Offy.

Deis sold the car to Jim Vernetti who in turn sold it to Jim Monaco for a restoration project. Fresnoan, Marvin Silva helped Jim restore the car.

Fresno's Dickie Deis in his V8-60. The "DC" in the front pusher is a reminder of Dick Cowan's ownership.

Jim Monaco's restored car at Ascot in the mid 80s.

Allen Heath is in the saddle for this race at Aurora Speedway. This 1946 picture is one of the earliest known photos of the car. Note the quarter elliptical springs in the front.

Chassis 04
duplicate

Tom Davey, from Denver, Colorado, contacted me about car he was restoring. In the course of the conversation he stated that he had seen the #04 stamped in the chassis of the Bob Van Buskirk V8-60 that ran in the R.M.M.R.A.

He heard that the car had been purchased as a kit car in 1946. Based in the radius rod pad location and dzus location it is difficult to understand how this could have been an early 1946 car.

Brad Bradford in the Bob Van Buskirk V8-60 at Pike's Peak Speedway.

Chassis 05   duplicate

It appears that Eddie Johnson ordered a K.K. chassis from the factory in late 1945, however he didn't take receipt of the car till nearly a year later!

Frank Kurtis wrote and told me who he believed the first ten original owners were. He thought Johnson received the 6th car.

The car was originally a red #44 V8-60. Later the car was outfitted with an Offy engine.

The car found its way to Ohio when Eddie relocated in Cuyahoga Falls.

According to Stan Lobitz, the car turned up on a farm in Ohio in the possession of a man named (?) Herman.

Wimpy Vorber appears to have been the next owner before selling the car to Bill Smith who transferred ownership to Dal Ewing and Stan Lobitz. When Ewing passed away Stanley purchased the car and found the #05 on the chassis.

Little Eddie Johnson poses in his newly acquired V8-60 powered Kurtis in 1947.

Chassis 05 duplicate#

My good friend, Tom Motter owned a chassis stamped #05. Jay Chamberlain was believed to have been the first owner.

The car was sold to Sam Dockery, who in turn sold the car to Kenny Olympius who ran it as a blue #66 Offy. Bob Bogan bought the car and ran it as a maroon V8-60 #63.

After Bob Bogan owned and campaigned the car it went through a succession of owners who simply passed the car along. They included, famed historian Jack Fox, Ray Lewis, and Russ Larson.

Tom Motter purchased the car as a restoration project in the early 1980s. Tom, with the help of Everett Duncan, did a beautiful restoration. The finished product was a pretty red and black #5 powered by a V8-60 engine.

In the early 1990s Tom sold the car to Marshall Matthews.

The Olympuis Offy with Bob Cortner in the ride.

Right: Tom Motter's restoration of the #05 chassis.

Below: Al "Cotton" Farmer from Fort Worth, Texas is seen in the blue #66 Kenny Olympius Offy.

Chassis 07

Southern California restorer, Rick Wold, believes this car to be the #21 Tuffanelli Offy driven by the likes of "Duke" Nalon and Tony Bettenhausen.

Rick feels that the car was sold to Brick Eicholtz after Tuffanelli got out of racing. After Eicholtz lost his life in the car it moved though the hands of Midwestern midget owners, Jack Drussa, Jack Yeager, Bill Mansell, Frank Wrzos and Carl Williams.

Rick believes Williams brought the car to California where he sold it to Jack London. London removed the Offy and sold the chassis to Nelson McKinney and Lou Bourdet, they ran it as a white #25 Chevy II. Ken Gandy and Willie Frasier were the last owners to race the car.

Rick purchased the car in the early 1980s and did a beautiful restoration job. The #21 car is now painted in the familiar maroon and gold colors of the "Tuffy" Offy.

Left: Dennis "Duke" Nalon guides the Tuffanelli Offy around the track in 1947.

Lower left: Brick Eicholtz lost his life in the former Tuffy Offy at Rocket Speedway in Ovid, Michigan.

Below: Rick Wold's restored Offy.

Chassis 08

The eighth chassis is the famous Lauren Bennett cream and red #8 Offy. Famed Eastern car owner Frank Curtis, from Hewlett, Long Island, bought the car when he came out for the 1946 Thanksgiving Day Grand Prix at Gilmore.

Curtis ran the car as a cream and red #8 Offy in A.R.D.C. with George Rice, Ted Tappett and Chet Gibbons driving.

Frank sold the car to Charlie Krick who only ran it once before selling it to Bill Yarroll. Yarroll ran the car as a plain white #8 and owned the car eleven years.

In 1961 the car was sold to Bill Jones as a parts car. Ed "Dutch" Schaefer bought it from Jones in 1961. Schaefer kept the car garaged until his death in 1978. Dutch's wife, Blanche Schaefer, sold it to Joe Donahue who sold it to Jim Witzler. Witzler ran it at vintage meets as a yellow #27 Offy. The car was sold to Ray Oldenburgh who tried to restore it to resemble the Curtis Offy but painted it blue and white instead of red and cream.

Rumor has it that after Ray Oldenburgh was killed testing the car it ended up in Chicago.

Above: A very rare photo of the #8 Lauren Bennett Offy taken on November 10, 1946 at Carrell Speedway. Aaron Woodard is the driver.   J.C. Coll.

Lower left: Eastern midget racing veteran Russ Klar in the Bill Yarroll Offy.

Lower photo: The immaculately maintained #5 and #8 Frank Curtis Racing team. Ted Tappett is in the #8 car and Chet Gibbons is in the #5.

Chassis 09

Several years ago I was contacted by Tommy Caruso from Massachusetts. He asked if I knew anything about a yellow and black #50 Offy Oscar Ridlon brought back from West 16th Street in 1955. I was not able to assist Tommy.

It appears Ridlon sold the car to Mike Scrivani who used it as a "parts car." When Tommy bought the car he started cleaning it up and found the chassis number to be 09.

Tommy sold the car to West Coast collector, Milt Jantzen.

Chassis 010

This is another car that is alleged to have been from the Lauren Bennett stable.

Bennett sold the car to Bernie and Lou Morgan in 1946. The Morgan Bros. were allegedly race promoters.

They ran the car until 1950. The car was usually painted yellow and red and carried the #3 with an Offy engine.

The third owner was a fellow named Baldwin. His first name is unknown. The car was maintained by Bob and Chuck Johnson and was driven by Potsy Goacher. Tragically Baldwin was killed in a highway accident and the car was sold in 1951 to Bob Sowle who ran the car as a red and black #7 Offy.

Bob had some very fine drivers in the car. Len Sutton and George Amick were just two of the men who wheeled this fine little machine. In 1958 Sowle sold the car to Bob Wilke.

The white #4 Offy reached its full potential during Wilke's ownership.

Don Branson won a 100 miler at DuQuoin in the car. Bobby Marshman also took a turn at the wheel in the car.

In 1968 Wilke sold the car to Gene Willman who ran the car in the Badger racing association.

Willman sold the car to John Hasseldorf who in turn sold the car to another Badger driver - Dean Billings. Billings sold the car to the Moore brothers of Moline, Illinois who are renowned for their collection of significant race cars.

Jerry Winston bought the car from the Moore brothers in 1993 and is restoring it to the Wilke colors.

Left: George Amick in Bob Sowle's Offy at DuQuoin.

Below: Bobby Marshman in the Leader Card Offy.

Chassis 11

This car is thought to have originally been Herb Richardson's hot little red and black #54 V8-60 that he campaigned in U.R.A. in 1947.

The following year Al Dean bought the car and ran it as a white #12 V8-60, chauffeured by Allen Heath.

The car was sold to Clay Walsh who ran it in B.C.R.A. in Northern California.

After Walsh retired he retained ownership of the car until he passed away.

In the early 1980s Martin Hagopian bought the car as a restoration project.

Martin restored it as the white #10 Al Dean V8-60.

The car was sold to Vintage car collector, Eddie Hegarty of San Pablo, California (1999).

Allen Heath does battle at Balboa in the Al Dean V8-60. Note the louver count and location on the Richardson and Dean cars. A perfect match.

Below: Two time Indy winner, Bill Vukovich seems to be pleased with the Herb Richardson V8-60.

Chassis 12

This car was owned and campaigned in the Midwest by Richard Heerboth who ran it as a Chevy II.

Ownership of the car was transfered to A.J. Todd who later sold it to Barton Montgomery.

Montgomery sold the car to Roger Adams who also ran the car in the Midwest.

In 1983 Roger sold the tired old chassis to a fellow named Joe Weiss, a High School shop teacher in Georgia, who planned to have his students dismantle and reassemble the car.

Chassis 13

This is one of the earlier East Coast restorations. Historian and photographer, Bruce Craig secured this car from A.R.D.C. driver Butch Walsh in the early 1980s.

The car has been restored and is painted in the familiar white and red trim associated with the Ronnie Householder stable.

Craig believes this car was first owned by Householder who debuted the unpainted car at the L.A. Coliseum in November of 1946 with Ralph Pratt doing the driving chores.

Householder campaigned the car in the Midwest.

According to Craig it went through a succession of owners before ending up on the East Coast. The car was purchased in 1998 by Harry Hunter.

A smiling Ronnie Householder in the #35 white and red Offy. This is believed to be his first K.K. midget.

Bruce Craig's pretty restored car carries the Householder colors but Bruce elected to put his own name and the #1 on it.

Chassis 16

This famous car was driven in the tough U.R.A. Red Circuit by the likes of Ruttman, Vukovich, Cantrell, Mantz and Zaring.

In its initial outing it was owned by Kittinger and Redding. The car was an ivory and red #98 V8-60. The car was driven by Ted Sizemore and Johnny Mantz.

In 1947 Redding dropped out of the picture and was replaced by ace mechanic Bill Stroppe.

In 1949 Stroppe became the sole owner of the car. With drivers like Bill Zaring and Billy Cantrell the car won the prestigious U.R.A. Red Circuit Championship.

Stroppe sold the car in 1952 to Joe Binter and Norm Innis. In 1953 they ran the car as a white and silver #5. Joe Binter bought the car in 1954 from Innis and ran it as a white and red #44 V8-60 until 1958. Leroy Martin and Bob McCoy bought the car in 1959. McCoy painted it blue and gold and numbered it #36. McCoy sold the car to Leroy Martin who ran the car as a cream and red #17X.

In 1965 Karl Raggio of B.C.R.A. bought the car and had it re-bodied by Jack Hageman.

In 1971 Raggio sold the car to Earle Bradford, who campaigned the car from 1971 to 1972.

Dave Thurston bought the car in 1975 and painted it white and blue with a #11.

After Thurston finished running the car it became a "parts car" and went through the hands of Paul Norris, Roger Bixler and Jerry Merrick.

Frank Moreira in San Leandro bought the car as a restoration project but never started it.

I bought what remained of the car and sold it to Marvin Silva of Fresno.

Marvin's love for this tired old veteran saved it from oblivion. His restoration is a work of art.

In 1996 Marvin sold the car to Ken Tucker of Los Angeles.

Above: Johnny Mantz in the Kittinger and Redding V8-60 in 1947.

Top: Bill Zaring twists the Stroppe V8-60 on his way to the 1949 U.R.A. Championship.

Lower Right: Joe Binter poses in the former Kittinger and Stroppe V8-60.

Lower Left: Northern California driver Karl Raggio in the car in 1965.

Chassis 017

Several two digit chassis numbers have an 0 prefix before the number. The only explanation is that it stood for Offy. However, I have never heard of a chassis marked with an "F" prefix for Ford.

Walter DeGenring purchased this car from John Kovas of Cleveland, Ohio. The racing history is not known.

Chassis 20

Don Murin of Lockport, Illinois gave me a brief history of this car.

It appears Mike Lividnik of Wisconsin was the first known owner. He ran the car as an Offy.

After Lividnik sold the car it went through the hands of Jim Patton, Joe Bergen and the Moore Bros.

When Bruce Moore sold the car to Don Murin he said he believed the car may have run with a V8-60 and later Chevy II while in the ownership of Bergen and Patton. He also believed Jerry Blundy and Bob Elliot were two of the car's drivers.

The dash tag reads 0-20-46 (1998).

Chassis 22

Tom Welch of Southern California purchased this V8-60 from Ralph Day.

The car is attractively restored as a blue and white #22 V8-60. The history of this car is unknown.

Tom Welch's restored #22.

Chassis 025

Once again we have a double digit number with a 0 prefix? Tom Motter bought this yellow #99 Chevy II from Tim Perkins in Iowa. Tim did not know the car's history.

Tom repainted the car red and white with Chevy II power. Motter sold the car to B.M.W. car dealer Ralph Day of Concord, California in 1996.

Right: Tom Motter's restored version of the 025 chassis.

Chassis 30

In 1946 Frank Vogel purchased chassis #30. The dash tag reads F-30-46.

The car was a pretty maroon and white #47 V8-60 driven by Frankie Cavanaugh and Johnny Smith, a formidable pair of B.C.R.A. drivers.

The car was sold to Eddie Wendt who successfully ran it as a white V8-60.

Jerry Boaz bought the car from Wendt and ran it for two years with a V8-60 engine. Later, Boaz put an Offy in the car and ran until 1971.

Super modified star Nick Rescino purchased the car from Jerry Boaz in 1976 and ran it as a yellow #86 Chevy II.

Rescino sold the car to Norm Rapp who sold it to Mike Mosekian for a restoration project. Mike sold the car to Jimmy Soares who still owns the car (1999).

Frankie Cavanaugh in the Frank Vogel V8-60 in 1946

A 1976 photo of Nick Rescino in the car formerly owned by Frank Vogel.

Chassis 31

Chassis 31 was allegedly owned by Doug Caruthers but it is doubtful that this is the car that Don Horvath lost his life in at Vallejo.

Chuck Porter did a first rate job of restoring and painting this attractive yellow and white #31 Offy.

In 1983 Chuck was driving the car at a vintage meet at Indian Dunes in Southern California when he crashed to his death.

Porters' relatives sold the car to Bob Larive in Pontiac, Michigan.

Doug Caruthers checks the car after the Don Horvath crash.

Chassis 032

The 32nd chassis was a famous one. Unlike many cars that went through a succession of owners this car was owned by a single person, Springfield, Illinois tavern owner Joe Shaheen. Shaheen owned this car from 1946 to 1979!

The car powered by an Offy engine was painted yellow and blue with a #39.

Joe's steady driver was Pete Romcevich, dubbed the "Flying Serb".

In 1991 George Boyd informed me he had purchased the car.

Pete Romcevich in the yellow and blue #39 owned by Joe Shaheen, tavern owner and promoter of the infamous "Little Springfield" Speedway.

Chassis 033

This information supplied by the current owner of the car, Jerry Marks, is rather non-specific and sketchy.

This car's first owner of record was Roy Thomas, followed by Clyde "Skee" Howard. His driver was Bob Cox.

Jerry purchased the car from Vance Cunningham.

Ned Kirkpatrick in the Thomas Offy at Cedar Rapids, Iowa in 1960.

Chassis 33

A V8-60 in the collection of famed photographer, Leroy Byers. Leroy said he got the car from Barney Manley and he believed it originally came from the Phoenix area.

Chassis 36

In 1990 Jim Aashe wrote to inform me he was the owner of a car with a dash tag that read 0-36-46.

The early history of the car is unclear, however, Aashe said it was owned by Lou Carver in 1959.

Carver ran the car as a red #4, Aashe was not specific about the engine.

Carver sold the car to Frank Conner who in turn transferred the ownership to Jerry Hardy.

Chassis 036

Ken Hillberg from Southern California is the current owner of a car that is stamped 036. Ken said that he knows nothing about the racing history of the car.

Chassis 037

Southern Californian vintage racing enthusiast, Joe Ricker purchased this car in Phoenix, Arizona.

Joe also said that he knows nothing about the racing history of the car.

Chassis 39

Frank Curtis picked up this car in California in November of 1946. The car became his famous red #5 Offy that was a "sister car" to the cream and red #8.

The car made its debut at Deer Park, Long Island in March of 1947 with Chet Gibbons at the wheel. Gibbons won his heat, the semi and the main event!

The car was sold to Latelle Miller and it was campaigned in 1948 by Johnny Rice and Bert Brooks. The car was painted yellow and blue and carried a #7 with Offy power.

Smokey Seccundo purchased the car in 1950 and put Johnny Thomson in the red and white #12 Offy.

Bob Hanrahan purchased the car in 1953. He painted the car reddish brown and white, tagged it with a #17 and had Tony Martino as the driver.

In 1957 Mel Nelson bought the car. The car was a blue #25 Offy. The car was driven by Chuck Arnold, Jiggs Peters and Ray Burke.

In 1959 Tim Kott purchased the car and changed the number to #51. Kott put Johnny Coy, Red Reigel, Roger Bailey, Al Keller and Bert Brooks in the car.

In 1961, the car was sold to Gene Ciabitari. The little blue Offy was called "Gene's Offy".

In 1969 Gene's other car was involved in an accident that took the life of young Larry Rice.

In 1980 the car was sold to Marty Himes who still owns the car.

Top: Chet Gibbons duels with Bud Tatro in the Frank Curtis #5.

Above: Johnny Rice in the blue and yellow #7 Latelle Miller Offy.

Lower Right: Jiggs Peters in the Mel Nelson car.

Left: Tough Tony Martino in his steady ride, the Hanrahan Offy.

Chassis 41

This chassis, purchased from Leonard Smith of Detroit, Michigan by Ben Cook, went through the hands of Freddie Charles, Jerry Maier, Bill Smith, Gordon White and me.

I believe Leonard Smith purchased the car from Bill "Booby" Logan who got it from the widow of Eddie Gdula.

I garnered most of my information from Al Hall, a man who worked on the Gdula Offy.

In the "Roar of the Mighty Midgets" Vol. 2 on page 132 there is a line alluding to Ralph Pratt's visit to California in the autumn of 1946 with Ronnie Householder to pick up two K.K. midgets.

We know that one of the K.K. midgets went to Householder. Was the other car earmarked for Eddie Gdula?

It is interesting to note that the previous car (Chassis 39) was picked up by Frank Curtis when he was in California at the same time. The car numbers are only separated by two digits.

Carl Forberg in the Lutes/Gdula Offy.

I am relatively certain that this car is the famous red #1 Lutes/Gdula Offy driven to countless victories by Ralph Pratt.

I sold the car to Mike Amato who in turn sold it to Marvin Silva of Fresno in 1995.

Marvin sold the car to Phil Fuller in Bowling Green, Ohio in 1997.

Fuller intends to restore it as the Lutes/Gdula Offy.

The legendary Ralph Pratt at the wheel of the Lutes/Gdula car in early 1947. This combination became nearly unbeatable in the Great Lakes and Ohio area.

Chassis 42

This car was apparently owned by Roger Newell before W.R.A. member Paul Larson got the car. Paul didn't have any information about the car's racing history.

Larson sold the car to John Ryals who in turn sold it in 1998.

Chassis 45

This famous orange #77 Offy was originally owned by Southern California resident Charlie Greenberg.

In 1947 Greenbergs wife sold the car to Kansas City's George Binnie when Charlie was in the hospital.

Binnie left the car as it was with the same paint and number. Binnie was a sensation in K.C.M.A.R.A. winning the 1947 Championship. Tragically, Binnie lost his life in this car on September 28, 1948.

The cars next owner, George Casey sold the car to Jack Hill who bought the car for his son, Mike. He also ran the car as an orange #77 Offy.

After Mike Hill, a popular and youthful S.L.A.R.A. Champion, lost his life in a racing accident at Charleston, Illinois on July 4, 1972 (in another car) the family sold the car to John Kieper.

Above: A very early photo of the Charlie Greenberg Offy. The driver is unknown.

Lower Left: Outstanding Kansas City midget racing star George Binnie in the former Greenberg car.

Below: Youthful Mike Hill gets a good ride out of the aging Kurtis.

Chassis 46

This car was owned by Bob Owen in 1971. It ran as a #15 Chevy II.

The car was sold to Michigan's Nick Hardie who transferred ownership to Freddie Fuhr. I assume Fuhr sold it to the current owner, Garette Dylewski.

Chassis 047

Jerry Weeks bought the car as a restoration project in 1996.

Jerry said that he could only trace this car back to 1962 when it was owned by Tommy Winchester.

Weeks believes that when Winchester moved from Southern California to the Midwest he sold the car to either Howard Linne or Harry Turner.

The car found its way to Don Reed (Reidelburger) in 1962. Apparently Reed owned the car from 1962 to 1965.

The last three owners appear to have been Ray Shilkulski, Dick Golden and Gene Coffing.

Chassis 48

This is a car that was allegedly owned by Ken Maish in 1946. Maish supposedly ran the car in B.C.R.A. as a white #44 Drake.

B.C.R.A. statistician, Jim Montgomery, has combed the records of that era and can find no record of Maish running a Kurtis. The records proclaim the Maish car to be a rail frame chassis.

Ken Maish sold the car to Howard Weiss who put a Ferguson tractor engine in the car. It was gray and red #38.

The last owner to actively campaign the car was Bill Newton.

He bought the car and painted it orange and white exchanging the "Fergie" with a Chevy II.

The car is currently in the possession of Chowchilla resident, Ed Roberts.

Chassis 49

This unusual car was built by and for Johnnie Parsons.

Leroy Byers said the dash tag was simply marked "Special Custom," however an article in *Open Wheel* February 1987 said the car's chassis was numbered 49 as well.

Johnnie Parsons sold it in Denver to Jim Urso until it found its way into Leroy Byers' collection.

Leroy had the pristine red #12 V8-60 in his garage for years until publisher Carl Hungness bought the car.

Hungness had his fling as a driver and decided publishing books was preferable to driving a race car so he sold the car to Lucky Mays.

Mays sold the car to Bud Marchman who restored it as a beautiful cherry red #12 V8-60.

Tom Davies in Leroy Byers V8-60 midget.

Chassis 050

In December of 1998 Freddie Chaparro contacted me to let me know that John Ryals had a K.K. midget with the chassis number 050.

I spoke to Ryals who said that the car originally came form the Midwest before being purchased by Sam Rodriguez, who raced in the R.M.M.R.A.

Rodriguez sold the #27 Offy to Myron Caves. Caves ran the car as a #84 Offy in 1967.

Ryals had the car for sale in 1999.

Don Meacham in the Myron Caves Offy.

Chassis 51

duplicate #

This V8-60 was originally owned by Bill Losey.

Losey sold the car to "Farmer" Ben Humke, a fabled car owner from Tulare in California's Central Valley.

In one of its prettier paint schemes it was yellow and black #1 when the famed Billy Garrett won the U.R.A. Championship in 1954 and 1955.

Humke sold the car to John Mosekian who ran the car as a blue #44 V8-60.

The next owner was Dan Avila. Tom Funkner was the last person to run the car in competition as a yellow and blue #66 V8-60.

Marty Mazman bought the car from Funkner in hopes that Ben Humke, who was poor in health, might be interested in restoring the car. Humke was not interested and Mazman sold the car to Toby Christopher. From Christoper the car passed through the hands of Vern Wortman, Jim Daly and Ray Alcarez.

In 1993 Alcarez sold it to Mike Mosekian who is the current owner (1998).

Hal Minyard in the famous "Farmer" Ben Humke car in 1959.

Chassis 51

duplicate #

Another #51 chassis appears to have been the Mack Offy owned by Frank Mack of Chicago, Illinois. Coincidentally the car was numbered 51.

The most memorable picture of this car shows George Mack, Frank's son, standing on Eb Yoder's chest with fists clenched after Yoder ran into him.

Al Craig bought the car in 1986 and sold it to Jim McDonald in 1990.

George Mack lets Eb Yoder know he isn't happy.

Left: George Mack at Soldier Field in Chicago.

Chassis 51

Duplicate #1

The final number 51 chassis was owned by E.C. Schneerer. He owned the car from the early 1980s until 1996.

Schneerer could not supply any information about the car's history, but one interesting fact is the dash tag which proclaims the car to be 0-51-46. This is my highest dash tag for the year of 1946.

The car was sold to Bob Roddemar in 1996.

Chassis 52

In 1996 George Boyd called to apprise me that he had purchased chassis #52 and it was in Bob Willey's shop being restored. I was surprised to learn that this was Bob Pankratz's red and black #32.

After Pankratz was injured at Bainbridge, Ohio in 1948 (in another car) he sold the car to Chet Miller. Miller put Mel Hansen in the car and he broke his back driving it at Motor Speedway in Detroit in 1949.

Miller sold the car to Pat Clancy, who ran it as a black #22 and hired Jimmy Davies as the driver.

In December of 1950 the car was stolen! The car did not surface until a picture of Ray Smith appeared in the *L.A. Times* on March 14, 1954, depicting his fatal accident at Capital Speedway in Sacramento.

After Davies reclaimed the car, Pat Clancy told him he could have it. Davies loved the car and referred to it as "Rosie's Little Box".

After he hooked up with Howard Linne in 1960 he won 46 U.S.A.C races and the 1960, '61 and '62 U.S.A.C. National Midget Championships!

Master car builder, Bob Pankratz, added his touch of genius to a stock Kurtis with amazing results! Perry Grimm rips it up at Balboa in 1946.

In 1966 Davies was killed in the car at Santa Fe Speedway in Illinois and the car was sold to his friend Les Scott.

Scott campaigned the car for years as a white, blue and red Offy. Les sold the car to George Boyd in 1996.

> Note: This might be an early 1947 or a late 1946 chassis. Dash tag information was not supplied.

Opposite Page Top: This car will always be identified with the great Jimmy Davies.

Left: Davies good friend, Les Scott, got the Davies' car and was the last person to campaign it competitively.

Chassis 54

This car was originally owned by Cy Thompson. The car was powered by a V8-60 with a 180 degree crank.

The car was sold to Ted Cornis who sold it to Roy Cook. Roy sold it to restorer, Ned Parsons. The car has been restored as an attractive cream and maroon #12 V8-60 as of 1985.

> Note: This might be an early 1947 or a late 1946 chassis. Dash tag information was not supplied.

The Ned Parsons car at Ascot in 1985. Parsons did a nice job of restoring this little V8-60.

Chapter Four

1947 Numbered Chassis

BUILT BY
KURTIS - KRAFT
— INC. —
LOS ANGELES
CALIF.   1947

—— **Chapter Four** ——

1947 Numbered Chassis

Chassis 57

This car is believed to have been the second K.K. owned by Rex Mays, the #4 white, red and black Offy.

It is significant because the dash tag was on the car when Don Conrad purchased it. The dash tag read 0-57-47, making it the earliest 1947 chassis *in my records*.

This means that Kurtis built no more than 56 cars in 1946.

The car was sold to Mike Fulper who sold the car to Bruce Nemeth in 1983.

An unidentified driver in the Mays Offy at Walsh Staduim.

Dick Hennesey ran this car as a #1 car piloted by Bobby Albert.

The car was sold to Jerry Willets whose cars were usually painted in a light blue and white color scheme.

Joe Donahue was the next owner. The car was a black and gold-leafed #98 Offy.

Joe May bought the car from Donahue and sold it to racing historian, Marty Himes. Marty ended up selling the car to Fred Bruckner who still owns it in 1999.

Shorty McAndrews in 1947 in an early Jerry Willets' Offy.

Chassis 60
duplicate

Oregon's Stan Muir originally owned this car. The car was sold to Pat Hargrove who ran the car in B.C.R.A. as a yellow #86 Offy.

Hargrove sold the car to O.J. Bellotti. Bellotti painted the Offy blue, white, yellow and red with a #20. His son-in-law, Jack Thompson, drove the car.

Cokey Williams owned the car after Bellotti. After its racing career ended it was sold to Mike Vukovich as a restoration project.

Mike abandoned the plan to restore the car when he read that his brother's K.K. Drake was being restored in Arizona by Bob Bamford.

Bob Bamford traded Mike the more desirable car, which Vukovich had owned, because he felt it was the right thing to do.

Bob was a kind and generous man that I counted as a friend. When he passed away the former Stan Muir Offy was nearly complete.

The current ownership and location of the car is unknown.

Top Right: Tommy Trader in the yellow #86 Pat Hargrove Offy.

Bottom Right: Bob Bamford had nearly completed the restoration project of the former Hargrove Offy when he passed away.

Chassis 60
duplicate

A second chassis numbered sixty is owned by John Gaspar. Nothing is known about the prior ownership or racing history of this car.

Chassis 66

duplicate #

A famous eastern Kurtis originally owned by Eddie Bourgnon, the car was painted turquoise and black #36. It ran as both an Offy and a V8-60.

Georgie Rice proclaimed this to be his favorite ride. He won the 1947 A.R.D.C. Championship in it.

The car was sold to Art Wohl who ran it as a V8-60 with the same colors and number.

After Wohl's ownership the car went through the hands of Tommy Cochrane, Derek Lewin and Pitt Kinsolving.

A restorer in Florida named Joseph Woolsey bought the car and restored it to the Bourgnon Offy colors.

Derek Lewin found his old car and purchased it from Woolsey. Derek sold the car to a collector named Bennett.

Bennett had a fire that destroyed most of the cars in his large collection. Fortunately the Bourgnon car escaped destruction.

Bill St. George bought the car and restored it in 1998.

Top Right: Georgie Rice in the Bourgnon Offy.

Bottom Right: Joseph Woolsey's restoration.

Chassis 66

duplicate #

In 1997 I was contacted by John Cyr who purchased a midget from the estate of the late Carrol Sleeper.

Mr. Cyr felt that the car could have been owned by Ed Czyzewski of Schenectady, New York.

The car was a four bar powered by a Falcon engine.

Chassis 68

This car was originally owned by Bob Wilke. This distinctive tan and red #45 Offy was driven by some of the finest driving talent in the Midwest.

Bob Wilke's mechanic, Joe Subjak, ended up with this potent iron.

The car has been owned for years by Bill Gunderson of Milwaukee, Wisconsin who has restored it to its original condition.

Gutsy Gordon Reid in the Subjak Offy indoors at the Chicago Amphitheater.

Chassis 69

This car is owned by Al Swenson in Chicago. Nothing is known about the prior owners or the car's racing history.

Chassis 70

Vintage car enthusiast, Jim Aashe, is the owner of this car. Unfortunately nothing is known about the car's racing history.

Chassis X71

The first X chassis that appears in my records belonged to Indy legend, Bill Vukovich.

It would be nice to say that Bill loved this pretty little Kurtis, but this was not the case. Vuky sold the red #4 Drake to Charlie Eich.

The car then made its way to a fellow named Eddie Phillips before being aquired by Bob Bamford.

Bob started restoring the car when he was contacted by Mike Vukovich who had heard that he owned the car (see chassis #60).

Bamford traded the car for the sixtieth chassis owned by Mike Vukovich.

Mike restored the car along with the famous Drake rail that his brother owned.

Mike passed away in 1996 but the car is still retained by the Vukovich family.

Above: Mike Vukovich did a beautiful restoration job on the X71 chassis.

Right: Bill Vukovich poses in his brand new K.K. Drake. The smiles turned to frowns when Vuky could not make the car work for him.

Chassis 72

Originally a Ford V8-60 with dash tag F-72-47, it is doubtful that Lysle Greenman was the first owner, however, he is the first recorded owner.

This was the famous red #20 Offy that ran in Southern California with Allen Heath as one of its drivers. After Greenman's ownership it was owned by Mike Kirk, Jake Mendoza, Wayne Taylor and Paul Evans.

In 1986 the car was bought by Paul Stewart of Phoenix, Arizona.

At present the car is a #85 Chevy II.

Allen Heath in the red #20 Lysle Greenman Offy at Gilmore in 1949.

Chassis 77

This is the first Kurtis - Kraft midget on my list that was stretched into a sprint car.

The current owner is Marvin Polansky from Southern California.

Polansky restored the car as a white #4 with a Sparks engine.

The car went through the hands of Vince Conze, Sarge Allen and Paul Larson before Marvin bought it.

The only information he had about the car was that it ran in the Midwest and was owned by a man named (?) Secriest.

Marvin Polansky's stretched midget.

Chassis X79

Apparently this car was originally a yellow #88 V8-60 when it raced in the Midwest.

A restorer in Indianapolis named Jim Mann is the first owner of record.

Mann sold the car to Jim Phillips who sold it to famed motorsports writer Brock Yates.

Yates had the car re-bodied by Jerry Weeks.

Chassis 86

Bob Peters of Joplin, Missouri owns this car. Unfortuantely, he like many owners of K.K. midgets, was unable to ascertain facts about the racing history of the midget.

The dash tag reads 0-86-47.

Chassis 85

One of the prettiest and hottest cars to grace the speedways of the east was the Tony Caccia Offy. It was so attractive that Frank Kurtis used a photo of it in one of his advertisements.

The car was a royal blue and white #1 Offy often driven by Rex Records, Georgie Fonder and Lloyd Christopher.

Caccia sold the car to Art Gottier, who, it appears, was not interested in the little K.K.'s general appearance.

Red Sanders was the last owner when it was still a competitive car.

Jim Sowers of Pennsylvania is the current owner (1996).

The immaculate Tony Caccia Offy with Georgie Fonder behind the wheel.

Art Gottier did not keep the car in the same condition as Tony Caccia.

Red Sanders in his orange #38 Offy.

Chassis X87

This car appears to have come from the Pacific Northwest before it came into the possession of Porter Goff.

Goff ran the car as a black and white #25 Offy in B.C.R.A. before selling it to Norm Rapp.

Norm Rapp ran the car for a couple of years. First, as a #10 then as a #16. Then he sold the K.K. to Frank Fiore.

Fiore ran the car as a white, red and blue #12 Offy. Fiore sold the car to the Roberts Brothers who painted it blue, white and black with a #1.

B.C.R.A. Champion, Ray Wise, bought it and raced it as a red and silver Offy.

Ralph Day purchased the car as a broker and sold it to the rock group "Pink Floyd" in 1983.

Top Right: The ageless Norm Rapp in the former Goff car.

Right: Chuck Booth in Frank Fiore's #12 Offy.   J.M. Collection

Below: Earl Motter in the #25 Porter Goff Offy.

Chassis 90

Chuck Stevenson ran this car as a #110 V8-60 before selling it to Arle Armstrong of U.R.A.

Armstrong ran this car as a #53 V8-60 in 1947. Arle sold the car to Fred De Orion who ran it as a circled #8. Johnny Boyd was one of his drivers.

Chuck Fraguero was the next owner before selling the car to Don Radbruch.

Radbruch ran the car for several years before transferring the ownership to Mason Cook.

After Cook, the car went through the hands of Jim Paniagua and Bill Horvath before restorer, Ron Ferguson of Omaha, Nebraska purchased the car.

Left: Don Radbruch in the former Stevenson car.

Right: Andy Guthrie in Arle Armstrong's #53 car.

Next Page Top: Chuck Stevenson in his #110 V8-60.
J.C. Collection

Left: Johnny Boyd in Fred De Orion's car.
J.C. Collection

Chassis X91

The first owner of this car was Dan Weist who ran it as a black and white #126 V8-60 in U.R.A. in 1948.

Bill Butters bought the car from Weist in 1957 and ran it as a #59 white Offy sponsored by Dean Van Lines. Danny Oakes was one of its drivers.

The car is now owned by Tom Rutherford. (Note: Rutherford said the number might be X97).

Perennial midget driver, Danny Oakes in Bill Butters little #59 Offy.

Chassis 91

Originally Carmine Tuffanelli's beautiful maroon and gold leafed #25 Offy. The car was sold to Jimmy Knight when Tuffanelli got out of the racing business.

Knight ran it as a black #2 Offy before selling the car in the east to Don Woods.

Jerry Willets bought the car from Woods. Dick Hennesey bought the car and sold it to Vinnie Parise. The next owners were Eddie Czyzewski, Stan Kurtis and Carroll Sleeper.

When Carroll Sleeper passed away the car was bought by Midwestern restorer Fred Johns of Detroit.

photos on next page

Chassis 92

It does not take Sherlock Holmes to figure out this was the "sister car" to the previous chassis. Legend has it that Harry Turner put together two Kurtis chassis for Tuffanelli at the same time.

This car ran as the Tuffanelli #23 Maroon and gold leafed Offy. When Tuffanelli sold his stable this car was bought by Bob Ellingham.

Ellingham told me the car was numbered 23 when he received it. Ellingham raced this car as a white #44 Offy.

Gil Michaels was the next owner. He also chose to campaign the car as a white #44 Offy.

The next owner was Ken Johnson who ran the car in Badger as a Chevy II.

Johnson sold the car to Wayne Branson who ran it as a red and yellow #71 Volvo powered car.

Wayne sold the car to Danny Frye in St. Louis and Frye promptly brokered it to Glen Jacobi in Pennsylvania.

A.R.D.C. driver, Doug Craig was the next owner. He sold the car to Paul Weisel who ran it as a #88 in A.R.D.C. The next owners were Kevin Scully and finally George Light who apparently bought it as a restoration project in 1982.

Stan Lobitz purchased the car from George Light in 1996.

Next page:

Top Left: Bob Ellingham in the former #23 "Tuffy" Offy.

Top Right: Wayne Branson in his own #71 Volvo.

Bottom: Carmine Tuffanelli's stable, including the #23 and #25 cars.

Chassis 91 continued

Hank Williams in Jerry Willet's car. The former #25 "Tuffy" Offy.

Jimmy Knight at the Grove in the former "Tuffy" #25.

Chassis 93

A controversial Detroit body shop owner Bill "Booby" Logan owned this black #16 Offy. Logan sold it to a man named De Coste who installed a Chevy II.

Little is known about the next three owners. Russ Snowberger's son, John, owned the car, then Bruce Boltinghouse and Bill Waite.

Waite ran the car as a white #87 in A.M.R.A. In 1986 Don Black bought the car as a restoration project.

Don sold the car to Phil Parnagian in California. It is being restored in Fresno by Marvin Silva.

When Bill Waite bought the ex - Logan car in 1986 it still looked like the same car.

Russ Congdon in Bill "Booby" Logan's black Offy.

Chassis X93

In 1999 Fred Johns from Michigan called to tell me he had a chassis that he bought in 1987 from a fellow named Art Range from Southern Illinois. Range couldn't remember where he got the chassis.

In March of 1999 Fred was checking the frame for marks and he found X93.

Chassis X96

George Grey of Rhode Island owns this car. Mr. Grey could not provide any information about the car's racing history, or prior owners.

Chassis X104

Rodger Ward drove this red #35 Offy, sponsored by, "Art Frost DeSoto". At that time the car was owned by Bill Matthews.

The car was sold to Ray Lattie who ran it as a Chevy II.

Jim Mack, John Cartwright and Johnny Rodgers were the next owners.

Rick Wold bought it as a restoration project before selling it to Marshall Van Tassel in 1982.

The current location of the car is not known.

Chassis 104

Walt Sweitzer bought this car in 1947. He ran it as a #128 V8-60 in U.R.A.

On June 3, 1950 Doug Grove lost life in the car at Bakersfield.

Sweitzer sold the car to famed car builder, Hank Henry. Hank also ran the car in U.R.A.

The car went through the hands of Bob Twitty, Zeke Maldonado and Dick Wallen.

B.C.R.A. driver Bob Johnson did a major update on the aging Kurtis.

Bob painted it black, gold, red and blue #73 and upgraded the V8-60 to Chevy II power.

Bob sold the car to Ron Skyrme who painted the Chevy II white and blue #73.

Skyrme sold the car to Lulu Russo who transferred ownership to Tom Blackwell. The bearded racer was the last person to campaign the car in competition as a blue and white #27 Chevy II.

In 1986 Arlen Kurtis bought the car for restoration purposes.

Top Right: Hank Henry in the former Walt Sweitzer Ford V8-60.

Lower Right: This 1975 photo of Ron Skyrme shows how the former Sweitzer V8-60 had evolved.

Chassis 105

This is owned by the Moore Brothers of Moline, Illinois. Nothing is known about prior owners or its racing history.

Chassis X106

Texas midget star, Lloyd Ruby, was the first owner of this car, originally powered by a Volker engine.

Lloyd sold the car to Harry Hull who put an Offy in it and painted it purple and white #15.

The cars next owner was another Texan, Bill Jones, who painted it red #45 with Offy power.

Bob Moore and Wayne Woodward owned the car after Jones.

Nate Ewing bought it for a restoration, but decided to sell it to Harold Seaman in 1986.

Seaman did a nice job of restoring the car to resemble the Hull Offy.

Chassis 107

In 1985 I was contacted by Bill Larzalere who informed me he had purchased one of the Eddie Meyer cars.

W.R.A. member George Chabot owned it before selling it to Larzalere.

Chassis 111

This is another undocumented car owned by E.C. Schneerer.

Chassis X108

Grant Marceau, of Rhode Island, contacted me in December of 1998 to apprise me of the fact that he had purchased this car from David Barnhart of Pittsburgh, Pennsylvania.

Barnhart said he bought the car in Indiana but couldn't supply the name of the person he bought it from.

The car's racing history is unknown.

Chassis X112

This well documented K.K. is currently owned by Tom Motter.

Jack Walters went into partnership with Frank Magarian on this kit car that ran as a pretty black, red and white #5 V8-60.

Magarian took over sole ownership, before selling it to Bill Correa.

Howard Segur Sr. ran the car as a #5 V8-60 in B.C.R.A. before selling it to Al Foppiano who put an Offy in the car and numbered it 79.

Roy Joyce bought the car and the red #54 Offy became Tim Joyce's first ride.

Bill Manley got the car from Joyce before selling it to Ralph Day.

Ralph, known as a broker for K.K. midgets sold the car to Marshall Matthews.

Matthews traded the car to Tom Motter for his fully restored Kurtis (chassis 05).

Top Right: Earl Motter in the Magarian #5 V8-60.

Bottom Right: Tim Joyce took his first midget ride in this Offy.

Chassis 113

Jim Aashe said this car was first owned by Bob Lockhart.

The car was a red and white V8-60 #75. Subsequent owners were John Gaul, Pancho Padilla, Ray Shilkulski, Bill Hack, and Jerry Hardy before Aashe acquired the chassis in 1990.

The last known owner was a fellow named Richard Freshman who said he had purchased the car in 1991.

Chassis X115

Australian, Malcolm Church purchased this chassis from Tim Stitley from Broobecks, Pennsylvania in 1990.

It was formerly owned by Bobby Albert who ran it as a white #2 with a 215 cu. in. Buick in S.M.R.C. on the East Coast.

The last owners who raced the car competitively were Ben Trimble and Denny Lott.

(Note: On the top of the frame member is stamped "K.K. 54". (The relevance of this stamp is unknown.)

Chassis X116

The racing history of this car in unrecorded. It is owned by Nick Hardie in Michigan.

Chassis X119

This Southwestern car was first owned by Tex West. He sold the car to Willie Hunziker.

Hunziker sold the car to George Turner who ran it as a red #1 Offy.

Scott Hunter was the next owner before selling it to Johnny Rodgers.

California vintage collector, Milt Jantzen acquired the car and sold it to Stan Goldstein.

Stan was very active at the W.R.A. vintage events for several years.

Several years ago Stan sold the car to the current owner, Mike Dewey.

Stan Goldstein's restoration.

Top Photo: Tex West in his own car in 1947.

Chassis 121

Leland "Buzz" Lowe bought one of the earliest K.K. chassis in 1946. He sold that car within months of buying it to Frank Armi who ran the car for many years.

The second car he purchased was a black #93 V8-60.

This car is especially interesting because Leland sent me a copy of his receipt for the car!

The receipt was dated July 24, 1947 showing the chassis number and tag information.

The tag read F-121-47.

Leland sold this car to Lloyd Van Winkle in 1948.

Van Winkle sold the car the next year to Don Christenson.

Jon Nickols bought the car in 1950 and kept it until 1979 when Ron Williams purchased it from him.

Leland Lowe found the car and purchased it in 1987.

It is easy to see how accurately Lowe restored the old warrior.

Leland "Buzz" Lowe in his new Kurtis at Carpenteria in 1947.

Chassis X124

Adolph Bonini's purple #98 K.K., powered by a Continental engine, has to be one of the most famous and recognizable cars in my records!

Bonini had Bob Allinger of San Jose, California tastefully alter the original K.K. lines.

When the car was sold to B.C.R.A., business manager, Jack London it reached the height of its fame.

London painted the "Bowes Seal Fast" sponsored car white, black and red #5 installing one of his potent Offy engines.

His drivers included Tony Bettenhausen, A.J. Foyt and Johnny Boyd.

A.J. Foyt staged many a duel with Parnelli Jones at Ascot Park driving this car in the early 1960s.

The next owner was Leo Wyrsch. He left the car the same color but it carried a number 99. It still had Offy power.

Lloyd Del Nero painted it pearl pink #7 with the venerable Offy still in place.

Dr. Walt Rore bought the Offy from Del Nero and ran it as a pearl white and blue #7.

Spike Carville bought the car, painted it yellow with the #60 and replaced the Offy with a Chevy II.

His driver, Victor Mencarini was involved in a terrible crash at Roseville, California that broke both his legs.

Gino Vaughan was the last owner to run the car competitively. It looked very much like the Carville car except it was #93.

Bill Botelho in Reno owns the car at the present and it has been restored by Harry Stryker (1999).

Top: A smiling Victor Mencarini at Roseville in the Spike Carville Chevy II.   J.M. Collection

Lower: Bob Machin in the Adolph Bonini Continental powered K.K.

Above: Jack London was an uncompromising car owner. His drivers were the best, one of them was arguably the greatest driver in the history of the sport...A.J. Foyt!
J.C. Collection

Chassis X125

Lysle Greenman's second Offy was a red #98 that he campaigned in Southern California.

It was a front runner, driven by "the little Dynamo", Walt Faulkner and George Amick.

Greenman sold the car to Jack London in Northern California who campaigned the car as a blue, red and white #98 Offy. It is strange that London owned chassis X124 and X125!

Lloyd Ridge bought the car from London and ran it as a red #98 Offy.

After Ridge's tragic suicide the car went to John Shanoian. The car remained a red #98 Offy from 1964 until 1969.

Gene Large acquired the car from Shanoian and left the car the same except for the number which he changed to #45.

John changed the number to #85. The car was still red with an Offy engine. Mibelli was the last owner to run the car in competition in 1978.

The last two owners bought the car with restoration in mind. Jim Wellington of Rennsport considered the idea but decided to sell the car to Ken Mann of Arizona in 1986.

Top Right: Davey Moses proudly poses in the London Offy.
J.C. Collection

Bottom Right: Driver Chris Luck in the John Mibelli Offy in 1978.
J.M. Collection

Chassis 128

Another stretched K.K. midget. This car competed in the Eastern U.S.A.C. sprint wars for years.

Jake Vargo owned the pretty maroon and white #35 Offy. The cars dash tag reads F-128-47. The car was owned by Bob Steiger and Stan Wilkins in 1989.

Chassis 130

This car is owned by John Doonan in Maryland. John didn't supply any information regarding previous owners or the car's racing history.

Chassis 133

Jim Ratelle called in 1991 to let me know that he had purchased a K.K. chassis from Jim Daly in Sacramento. He didn't know any of the other owners or the racing history of the car.

Chassis 134

The MacLeod Offy #20 was the Kurtis in the famous two car team.

This maroon and white #20 Offy is the car that helped establish Johnny Thomson as a future star.

The car's next owner, Blackie La Macchia, aka Bobby Black, ran it for years as a red and black #20 Offy. La Macchia, still owns this once potent iron.

Top Photo: "Blackie" La Macchia ran the ex - MacLeod Offy for years. He still owns the car.

Bottom Photo: Johnny Thomson won the New England Championship in this car in 1948.

Chassis 135

One of the many cars in the Ken Hickey stable. Ken wrote to tell me this was one of the cars he owned. The I.D. tag read F-135-47.

Chassis 138

Although Roscoe "Pappy" Hough owned quite a few cars most of them were rather well used rails!

"Pappy" Hough was a colorful figure whose drivers included Bill Schindler, Vernon Land, Steve McGrath and Art Cross.

This car is the #81 K.K. sold to Charlie Hophan, driven by Vernon Land and Charlie Musselman.

Jim Mann was the next owner of record before selling the car to John Keiper in 1987.

Vernon Land in the Hough Offy.

Carl Miller in Charlie Hophans Offy. The points of identification are obvious on this Kurtis. Twenty - six louvers on the hood and a distinctive "cow catcher" front pusher!

Chassis 139

A well known car in B.C.R.A., this was originally a maroon and white #7 V8-60 owned by George Bignotti.

Bignotti sold the car to 1949 Indoor Midget Champion, Bob Sweikert. Sweikert numbered the little V8-60 #140. On the side of the car he painted "The Old Goat".

Sweikert sold the car to Del Black who ran it as a white #7 V8-60.

When Bob Valencia took possession of the car he painted it maroon, numbered it 52 with a V8-60 engine.

The next owner, Roy Newman campaigned it as a white #32 V8-60. Newman sold the car to Rich Walsh who painted the car blue and white and gave it a #92. The car was still V8-60 powered.

Leo Bonari bought the car from Walsh and installed a Chevy II in the chassis and numbered it #197. Charles Pollack purchased the car from Bonari and campaigned it as a blue #63 Chevy II.

The last owner to race the car was Bob Allen who painted it brown and yellow #91 with the same Chevy power.

Mike Mosekian bought the car for restoration purposes and sold it to former B.C.R.A. driver and Business Manager, Tommy Morrow.

Tom sold it to Jim Sullivan in Los Angeles in an unrestored condition in 1983.

Bill Amberg in Del Black's white #7.   J.C. Collection

Frankie Cavanaugh in the George Bignotti V8-60.

Chassis 141

Dennis Gage sold this stripped chassis to Jim Daly. Jim in turn sold the car to Pete Bray in 1990. Nothing is known about the car.

Chassis 142

The original owner of this car was Jerry Willets. Although Willets had several blue and white Offies with the #41 this car is alleged to be his first.

Vic Henkels bought the car and has restored it beautifully in the familiar Willets' colors.

Vic said it had Willets' original Offy engine #172 in the car.

A youthful Al Keller in an early photo of Jerry Willets' car. Teammate, Johnny Ritter seems happy to be driving the rail.

Chassis 145

Ken Hillberg owns this car. He bought the car new and raced it until 1979!

Allen Heath, George Amick and Billy Cantrell were some of the men who drove his yellow #17 car.

The car was originally a V8-60 but Hillberg tried many different engines including an Offy, Buick V6, Buick V8 and even an outboard.

Ken Hillberg's #17 car at El Toro. The driver is Ray Jimenez, designer of the Arias engine.

Chassis 147

K.C. Breslauer, the editor and publisher of the defunct publication, *"Auto Racing Memories and Memorabilia"*, owned a K.K. that he bought in the Midwest. The only information he had, that would indicate who the former owner might be, was the name "Lothe Chevy II", painted on the hood.

Chassis 150

Chassis 150 was originally purchased by Elza Bynum.

The car numbered eighteen with Offy power was sold within weeks of its purchase to M.A. (Marcus and Alfred) Walker.

The car retained the #18 and scored numerous victories in the Southwest with "Joltin" Jud Larson at the wheel.

In an ad in N.S.S.N. the Walkers gave the dash tag number 0-150-47. The ad went on to say that the car was built in September of 1947.

Both of their Kurtis' were sold to Bill Meers of Oklahoma City in 1950.

Chassis 150 or chassis 354, the second M.A. Walker Offy, was stretched to a sprint car by Buzz Barton in 1951.

"Joltin" Jud Larson in the M.A. Walker Offy - a tough combination to beat!

Chassis 151

Fresno's lead footed cotton farmer, Norm Girtz bought this Kurtis in 1947.

The car was painted maroon #39 with a V8-60 engine, a bit out of place for someone strongly identified with the Drake engine.

Girtz sold it in 1948 to fellow Central Valley resident, Ray Messer.

The car, a gray and red V8-60 was usually in the top five at the end of the season in U.R.A.

Racing great, Bill Vukovich was one of Messer's drivers.

The car was sold to Dennis Johanson who ran the car in B.C.R.A.

Johanson's car was stolen and ended up in Stockton, California.

B.C.R.A. Vintage division member, Mike Mosekian located the car and purchased it in 1998.

Bill Vukovich on the inside in the Ray Messer V8-60. Note the "G" in the front pusher of the former Norm Girtz car. Outside of Vuky in the #2 Stroppe V8-60 is Bill Zaring (see chassis #16).

Chassis X152

Well known in A.A.A. midget racing in Southern California this little red #22 Offy was owned by midget racing pioneer, Dominic "Pee Wee" Distarce.

The car was sold in the Pacific Northwest to Claude Lathrop. Lathrop ran the car as a black #2 Offy sponsored by "Clear Creek Trout Farm".

The car was driven by Don Olds and Mel McGaughy.

In 1950 it finished second in Northwest points and became known as the "Deuce".

Sid Carr was the next owner before selling the Kurtis to driver Jim Glenn.

Jim ran the Offy in his familiar blue and white colors. The car carried his equally familiar #61.

Jerry Eberle bought the car and installed a V8-60 engine and numbered it #42.

The next owners were; James Hendricks, John Gregg, Bill Seidelman and Ray Basset before the current owner, Lee Elwell, bought the car as a restoration project.

Dominic "Pee Wee" Distarce poses with driver Bill Homeier at Gilmore in 1948.

Chassis 154

It is wonderful to find someone who really cares about preserving the history of a car.

Pat Long of Thousand Oaks, California has been researching the history of his car since he bought it from Jimmy Soares in 1991.

Soares purchased the car from Newt Garrett, who campaigned it in B.C.R.A.

Jim intended to restore the car.

Through Pat Long's diligent efforts it was discovered that in the 1950s George Shilala acquired the chassis from a driver or owner from the Midwest named (?) Kelly.

He brought the car to George's shop, to be straightened after it had been badly damaged in a crash.

Shilala told him he would build him a new chassis and take the old chassis as partial payment.

Later he repaired the old Kurtis chassis for Owen Herron who ran the car in Southern California from the mid '50s until 1967.

He transferred ownership to Newt Garrett in 1972.

Chassis 158

A K.K. that Ralph Day had in his inventory was purchased from Southern California car owner Louie Roeder.

Roeder ran the car in U.R.A. and later ran the car as a blue and orange #37 Chevy II in U.S.R.C.

Chassis 159

The dash tag reads 0-159-47. The earliest owner is Ken Van Woert, who sold the car to Charlie Springer. Springer ran the car as a #18 V8-60 in 1948.

Charlie Springer relinquished ownership to Howard Segur.

It is believed Howard's son still owns the car.

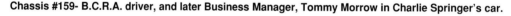

Chassis #159- B.C.R.A. driver, and later Business Manager, Tommy Morrow in Charlie Springer's car.

Chassis 160

Ed Petshaver originally owned this 1947 K.K. that he campaigned infrequently with B.C.R.A.

This light blue V8-60 used its chassis number 160 as the car number!

Between 1947 and 1949 Ed put some formidable drivers behind the wheel of his clean little machine, drivers like Henry Banks, Woody Brown and Freddie Agabashian.

This was Ollie Johnson's first K.K., purchased in 1955. He ran it as a blue and white #96.

Jim Lawson bought the car from Ollie in 1959 and ran the blue and white V8-60 until 1961.

Chuck Fulton purchased the car from Lawson and sold it to Don Carmichael, the last man who raced the car as a red and black #11 V8-60 in 1963.

Below: Buck Whitmer in the clean Ed Petshaver V8-60.

Chassis 161

Jack O'Brien ran this pretty blue and yellow V8-60 #5 in B.C.R.A. with the legendary Bob Sweikert twisting the wheel.

After O'Brien was forced to re-locate to Southern California he sold the car to Stan Brooks.

Johnny Baldwin, Bob Machin and Bob Veith were a few of the extraordinary chauffeurs who drove this car when it was a yellow #1 V8-60.

Bill Shaw was the next owner before selling the car to Marvin Silva in Fresno.

Silva sold the car to fellow restorer, Milt Jantzen and he sold it to former driver, Dickie Reese. Reese sold the car back to Jantzen who re-sold the car to Eli Vukovich.

The current owner and location are unknown.

Top Photo: Bob Machin posing with his "hardware" in Stan Brooks' car.

Below: Jack O'Brien's clean '60 with Woody Brown in the saddle.

Chassis 163

Emil Andres sent me a copy of his receipt from Bob Wilke dated December 11, 1947.

It states that the car he bought possessed chassis #163 and the Offy engine is serial #293.

Emil said he could never get the car to handle and he sold it to Tony Bettenhausen.

This was his clean white and red #1 Offy. Pretty cars are not always good handling cars.

Tony couldn't get the car to behave and he ended up selling it.

The current owner is not known.

Tony Bettenhausen in his own immaculate Offy.

Chassis 164

In a letter dated 1996, Ken Hickey told me this was a car he had owned.

The dash tag read 0-164-47.

Chassis 165

Many people associate a particular car with a driver. This was the famous white, red and black V8-60 owned by Charles "Dutch" Hurd in U.R.A.

The inimitable "Seattle Screwball" Allen Heath was the car's steady driver annexing the 1958 U.R.A. Championship in it.

The car was sold to John Schmick and he sold it to Lloyd Hendrikson, the owner in 1986.

Allen Heath will always be remembered for his grit and determination. Devastating injuries and the loss of his left hand in a sprint accident couldn't slow his career.

Chassis 170

This car, originally a #90 Offy, was owned by Fred Maier and driven in A.R.D.C. by Russ Klar.

Maier sold the car to Ed Darrell in 1950. Darrell ran the car for years with a formidable list of drivers that included Bill Randall, Bert Brooks, Joe Barzda and Al Herman. The blue #83, called the "Darrell-Villa Offy" in honor of his long time pal, George Villa, was never in contention as the prettiest car in A.R.D.C. The faded blue paint was nicked and pitted, strangely it was one of my favorite cars!

In September of 1959 the car was involved in a horrendous accident during the running of the Trenton 100 miler. Bert Brooks was badly burned when the car hit the first turn wall and flipped. Bert came rolling and tumbling out of the car down the banking of the track, with no visible flames emanating from the alcohol fire.

Soon emergency crews discovered the reason for his grotesque gyrations, the fire was put out and he was taken to the hospital.

Shortly after the accident Darrell sold the car to Carl Miller who ran it as a black #55 V8-60.

Miller later put an Olds engine in the car.

The current owner, Bill Goodfellow, bought the car from Don Dadswell (1998).

Above: Lanky, Bill Randall in the Ed Darrell Offy at Flemington, New Jersey in 1957.

Below: Harold "Pickles" Bickelhaupt in the Fred Maier Offy. The name was funny but his driving was no joke!

Chassis 172

This was the chassis under Ernie Casale's beautiful blue and white Offy with the Fred Glass body so ably driven by Billy Garrett, Edgar Elder and Earl Motter. Sadly, this chassis is totally rusted away!

The car was sold to Joe Bertoncini who ran it as a red and white #17 Offy.

Apparently Bertoncini built or bought a K.K. copy and left the original chassis out in the elements.

Marvin Silva now possesses what remains of tne historic car.

Top: Billy Garrett in the white and blue Ernie Casale Offy.

Chassis 176

This was a former Jack London Offy that was purchased by Moe Goff.

Goff sold the car to Bob Spoo and Gene Gurney. Spoo and Gurney sold the car to Lenny Esposto who ran it as a white, purple and black V8-60 and Chevy II. 1959 B.C.R.A. overall and 1960 Indoor Champion, Davey Moses, was Esposto's driver.

Moses, a talented and promising driver, lost his life in the car in the 1/2 mile at Capitol Speedway in 1960 at Sacramento.

Lenny owned the car until 1998 when he sold it to John DiMartini in 1998.

Davey Moses and Lenny Esposto look pleased with their trophies.

Chassis 178
duplicate

This was one of Shorty Burns' Offies. Burns sold the car to Rod Smith. Smith transferred ownership to Gus Sohm who ran it as a beautiful white and gold #92.

It is currently owned by a fellow named Mick McMillen.

Dwight Brown in Gus Sohm's well maintained Kurtis.

Chassis 178

duplicate #

The dash tag reads 0-178-47. Eldon Ellis has owned it since 1982.

Mr. Ellis did not have any information about the car's history, or previous owners.

Chassis 182

Jim Di Marco put this black #98 car together in 1947.

I remember seeing Di Marco drive this car at Freeport Stadium in 1956.

Di Marco sold the car to Ray Brown in 1960. The car then went through the hands of Jerry Willets in 1962, Vinnie Parise in 1965, Charlie Gardner in 1966, Bill Sowle in 1968 and Fred "Meatball" Orlando in 1969.

Al Molinaro now owns the car.

Chassis 185

Otto Bowden owned this car in 1982. The dash tag read, 0-185-47.

Mr. Bowden didn't supply me with any history, or the names of the previous owners.

Chassis 188

The Allen Kaminski Offy was well known in the Midwest. It was painted white and maroon #12. The dash tag reads 0-188-47.

The car was sold to Lee Austin and then Lee Elkins of McNamara fame.

It is not known if this was the McNamara #73 or #83 car.

In 1983 it came into the possession of Charles Bell in Georgia.

Gene Tierney bought the car in 1992 and restored it in the familiar Kaminski colors.

Top Photo: The restored version of the Allen Kaminski Offy.

Bottom Photo: Potsy Goacher in the McNamara Offy.

Chassis 197

Bob Willey told me his father, Al, was the original owner of this car. Al was a Kurtis - Kraft dealer who displayed the car at fairs to promote K.K. midgets.

The car was a red and white #12 V8-60. The current owner of this car in unknown.

Johnny Hobel drove this neat V8-60 and years later had Bob Willey make a replica for him (see chassis #02).

Right: Johnny Hobel in Al Willey's V8-60.

Chassis 199

This is believed to have been another Lee Elkins midget. It is an odd coincidence that chassis 188 and 199 are both reputed to be cars owned by the famous car owner.

Once again it is unknown if this was the #73 or #83 McNamara Offy.

This car is currently owned by John Palmer of Massachusetts. The car is a red #32 Offy.

Chassis 201
duplicate

A car owned by Dick Knudson carries the same number as the previous car. The dash tag reads 0-201-47.

Dick owned the car in 1983. Mr Knudson didn't supply the names of the previous owners and he was unaware of the car's racing history.

Chassis 201
duplicate

This is the most unusual number I have come across.

This dash tag reads 03-201-47. The current owner, John Howard made a rubbing of the number for my records.

I can't imagine what the meaning of an 03 could be.

Nothing is known about the car and Mr. Howard didn't supply the names of any of the previous owners.

John has restored it as an attractive reddish orange #25 V8-60.

A trailered shot of John Howard's #25 V8-60.

Chassis 208

duplicate #

Johnny Pawl sold this black K.K. to Bob Werden and Paul Mergens. It ran as a red, white and blue #69 Chevy II.

In 1970 Bob Anderson bought the car. Seventeen years later he sold it to Spike Gillespie in 1987.

An action photo of the #69 Werden and Mergens Chevy II taken in the late 1960s.

Chassis 208

duplicate #

Emil Andres favorite car was the familiar, well maintained white and blue #51 Bayer and Anderson Offy.

The car is now owned by Bill Jones in Texas. Bill has restored it to the Bayer and Anderson colors with Offy power (1996).

Emil Andres in his favorite midget ride, the Bayer and Anderson Offy in 1948.

Chassis 212

Thomas Scheck [aka] "Shorty" Burns was the original owner of this car before selling it to Gus Sohm.

It was probably the #93 Offy that Dick Word drove. Sohm ran this car as his white and gold #93 Offy.

Mick McMillen, the current owner of Sohm's other car, owns this car as well (1989).

Crew Chief Sonny Knepper and a bespectacled, Arnie Knepper in the Gus Sohm Offy.

Chassis 213

This chassis came into the possession of the late Ollie Johnson in the mid 1980s after going through the hands of Sarge Allen, Paul "Punky" Grosso, Dave Martin and Bill Mayhew.

Historically, nothing is known about this car. After Ollie Johnson's death the car was sold to current owner, Bob McMurtry (1998).

Chassis 215

This car, 0-215-47, is owned by Harry Stryker in Washington State.

The car's history is unknown. As a result Harry elected to restore the car to resemble the car he campaigned in B.C.R.A. The restoration is beautiful!

Chassis 223

Bob Johnson of Puyallup, Washington sold this Offy to Les Stark. From Stark it went to Ralph Day before being acquired by W.R.A. member, Bob Ware in Southern California.

Nothing is known for certain about the car's racing history. Bob has painted the car cream #15 with an Offy engine.

The Offy owned by Bob Ware in the pits at Ascot in the mid 1980s.

This concludes the section on numbered chassis for the production year 1947.

In 1948 the magic that surrounded midget racing, in the post-war period, began to fade. This is evidenced in the 1948 production figures.

Chapter Five

1948 Numbered Chassis

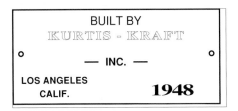

— Chapter Five —

1948 Numbered Chassis

Dash Tag 230

Chassis 0-230-48 is not a chassis at all, merely a dash tag in the possession of Nate Ewing.

I include this because it is the lowest chassis number I have discovered in 1948.

Chassis 233

This chassis is reputed to be one of the many K.K.'s owned by Ronnie Householder.

Dale Swaim ran the car as a white #44 Offy. The next owner was Clyde Lowther who ran it as a blue #3 Offy.

In 1986 Bill Smith in Pennsylvania was restoring the car to sell.

Dale Swaim in his white #44 Offy.

Chassis 236

In 1999 Australia's Malcolm Church wrote me to tell me he bought a chassis from Don Kischell.

The car was believed to be the famous Hart Fullerton "Kopper Kart" Offy in which Eddie Haddad lost his life at Gilmore on October 21, 1949.

Church said this also might be a "spare car" owned by Fullerton.

The word, DUNHAM is stamped on the rear crossmember. Perhaps Larry Dunham had something to do with the car?

Top: Eddie "The Villain" Haddad in the car when it was #3.

Below: Haddad in the "Kopper Kart" as it was best remembered.

Chassis 237

Historically important because we know the date this famous car was purchased. This car, 0-237-48, was purchased by Ken Hickey on February 27, 1948.

Hickey sold the car many years ago and bought it back in 1987 as a restoration project.

In 1995 he sold it to Tom Fitzgerald.

Midget master, Georgie Fonder, in one of the Hickey Offies.

Chassis 239

Jim Witzler bought this car in 1995. Originally owned by Art Olle from Fairport Harbor, Ohio the car ran as a white #16.

Al Silver purchased the car from Olle. It is doubtful that this is the famous #7 ex-Carter Offy.

The next owner was Don Rosenow before Dave Bixler who transferred ownership to Witzler.

Buddy Martin in the Don Rosenow Fergie called, "The Dutchess".

Chassis 243

In 1991 I received information from Jack Layton in Florida who had the car. Mr. Layton didn't provide any information about prior owners or the car's racing history.

Chassis 251
duplicate

According to Tom Kalkofen, the current owner, this car was raced by Ed Zalucki as a Chevy II.

Mr. Kalkofen couldn't supply any other substantive information about the car's prior history.

Chassis 251
duplicate #

In 1948 Bill Randall drove from Massachusetts to California to pick this car up for Jack Rose.

Randall drove it in 1948 and in '49 Johnny Thomson ran it with great success.

Rose sold the car to Dick Brown. The car was painted cream and red #5.

In 1956 Brown sold the car through Johnny Pawl to Ashley Wright. It was campaigned as the white #1 Offy with the black splash on the tail. Bob Gregg was the driver.

Wright repainted the car brown with a gold-leafed splash #8.

In 1958 Ashley sold the car to Helen and Don Bailey when he decided to get out of the "midget business" and run a champ dirt car.

The car, known as the Hel-Don Special, was still Offy powered and it was re-numbered #62.

The Baileys sold the car to Lou Buchari who ran it as a Maroon #12 and #33 Offy.

After an accident at Thompson, Connecticut, Buchari parked the car until it resurfaced as a black and orange #29 owned by Bill Davis.

Stan Lobitz bought the car in 1990s.

Top Photo: Bill Randall in the Jack Rose Offy.

Center Photo: Bob Gregg in the Wright Offy.

Lower Photo: Dickie Brown in the former Rose car.

Chassis 252

This red, white and blue #20 Offy was owned by Gays Biro.

Tragically, Biro, who had a very active, rough and tumble existence as a driver, lost his life in this car at a vintage meet running at less than 30 M.P.H.!

The car is on permanent display in the Eastern Museum of Motor Racing.

The car in which Gays Biro was fatally injured at Williams Grove in a vintage exhibition race.

Chassis 254

Rick Stewart of Phoenix, Arizona owns this chassis. The history is unknown.

Chassis 255

One of the most famous V8-60 midgets produced by Kurtis - Kraft.

This car was originally owned by Jess Beene. The little black and white #21 sponsored by Bardahl was driven by legendary Johnny Baldwin.

Beene sold the car to Paul Meyer who sold it to Dean Holden who ran it as a white and blue #9 that was a many time winner at Fresno's Kearney Bowl.

Johnny Baldwin bought the car from Holden and campaigned it as an orange and black V8-60. Jimmy Montgomery bought the car from Baldwin in 1961 and raced it until 1982 as a V8-60 and an Offy.

Jim still owns the car which is being restored by Gary Bulfinch (1999).

Middle Photo: The great Johnny Baldwin in the former Beene car.

Bottom Photo: A youthful Jim Montgomery stands next to Bob DeJong, seated in his car in 1961.

Chassis 258

This car was originally owned by Bill Nimzik before it was sold to Bill Lynch.

Lynch ran it as a cream and blue #10 Offy. The car was driven by Henry Renard.

The car's next owner was Andy Furci who ran it as the Hazzard Offy #10.

Furci sold the car to John Lalli who painted it yellow and red #10. It was sponsored by Trailways Van Lines.

Bill Abernathy was the last owner to campaign it before Jim Barclay bought and restored it to the Lynch colors. This is a beautiful restoration.

The current owner is unknown.

Above: Henry Renard in the Lynch Offy.

Above Right: The Jim Barclay Restoration of the Lynch car.

Right: 1950 Indy Winner, Johnnie Parsons in the Lalli Offy at Old Bridge N.J. in 1958.

Chassis 261

In the early 1980s I received a picture of a white and red #11 K.K. with a Buick V8 engine! The car was in the possession of Robert Wright from Ohio. The dash tag read F-261-48. Wright said the car belonged to Greg Mahoney before him.

Vigil Welsh was the first known owner of the car, which had one of the most impressive records of any car in the Midwest and carried the Red and White #11.

The Elwood, Indiana car owner had Eddie Yeager as his main chauffeur until 1957 when Yeager quit after a wild flip at Alexandria, Indiana. The car was powered by a Ford V8-60 until 1963, when Welch installed the Buick.

Two time CORA Champion, Gene Rodgers won the 1963 CSRA Championship in the car. Ed Watson remembers Rodgers running the car as late as 1966.

Rick Kerr in the Virgil Welch V8-60.

Chassis 262

Hud Meyer reported this number was on the dash tag of the famous red and white #25 Offy owned by Ray Plakstis and driven by Mike Nazaruk.

Mike Nazaruk in the #25 Ray Plakstis Offy and teammate, Lloyd Christopher in the #15 Offy at Avon, Connecticut in 1948.

92

Chassis 266

George Bignotti was the first owner of this blue and white #154 V8-60 driven by Freddie Agabashian.

Bignotti sold it to Tex McClanahan who ran it as a maroon and white V8-60 from 1950 to 1955 before selling it to Norm Rapp.

Rapp ran the car from 1955 until 1959. He sold the car to John Estes in 1960.

Estes painted the car yellow #74 with a V8-60 engine.

In 1963 Joe McGee purchased the car and ran it for a single season as a black #37 V8-60.

Nelson Kinney bought the car from McGee and raced it as a red and black Chevy II.

In 1965 Bob Lewis purchased the car from Kinney and raced it as a red and black #55 V8-60, for one season.

Dave Logan bought the car in 1965 and ran it as a white and blue #31.

Logan transferred ownership of the V8-60 to Leroy Geving in 1970 and he, in turn, sold the car the following year to Roland Lokmor.

Lokmor put a Chevy II engine in the car and ran it until the early 1980s in B.C.R.A.

Mike Mosekian bought the car and sold it to Jimmy Soares in 1986.

Soares still owns the car (1999).

When Freddie Agabashian and George Bignotti teamed up it was a tough combination to beat!

Chassis 267

Historian and author, Gordon White, saved this famous car from oblivion.

It was the original Roy Hagedorn black and red #9 Offy before being bought by Tassi Vatis.

Tassi ran it in A.R.D.C. with the same colors, number and Offy power plant. Tony Bonadies was his steady driver annexing a number of wins at the tricky Freeport oval.

Ken Anderson bought the car and painted it coral pink and white, numbered 21 with an Offy engine. Bobby Boone was one of his drivers.

Al Monast was the next owner. He ran the car as a #19 powered by an Offy, with Dickie Brown at the wheel.

The car was sold to Ken Hickey and in the following years passed through the hands of Bruce Turgeon, Dorsey Truitt (#92 Offy, 1971), Dick Soubirou and Fred Schell who ran it as a black and orange #72 Chevy II, before finding its way to Gordon White.

Gordon not only runs the car at vintage meets but he also runs the car at the Bonneville salt flats at speeds approaching 160 M.P.H., fast enough to set a new Worlds Record in its class!

In a near tragedy, Gordon's legs were badly burned when his engine let go at Limerock, Connecticut in 1997. Fortunately Gordon made a full recovery, and his Offy engine survived to run again!

Top Photo: Bobby Boone in the Anderson Offy.

Center Photo: Gordon White's beautiful restoration of the former Hagedorn Offy.

Right Photo: Johnny Kay in the Roy Hagedorn Offy at Norwood Arena in Massachusetts in 1952.

Chassis 272

duplicate #

This chassis was originally owned by Hanley "Cadillac" Booth, an uncle of the Booth brothers, Jay and Ernie. The car was a #98 V8-60 painted white and red, in a style not unlike the Kittinger Redding car.

Booth hired several drivers to pilot the car including Marcel St. Cricq, Jay Booth and Cotton Musick.

Booth, a double amputee, with a missing hand and foot, tried to drive the car himself. He managed to tip it over and skin himself up pretty badly! At this point Booth sold the car to Stan Smith.

Smith sold the car to Walt Portis. Portis conveyed ownership to a man in Texas named (?) Popping. Popping ran it as a red and white #23 Offy, but the car's most famous days were yet to come.

Lloyd Snook acquired it, and with the addition of some body work by Wayne Ewing, it was transformed into a unique looking car. Johnny Tolan and Billy Mehner were two of the drivers who chauffeured the sleek #65 car for Lloyd.

Snook transferred ownership to Danny Frye. Frye sold it during the Winter racing series in Florida to Ernie McCoy and Ed "Dutch" Schaefer.

Nate Ewing got the car after it ceased to run competitively with the hopes of restoring the car.

Nate abandoned the project and sold the modified Kurtis to Jim Kilgore in North Carolina.

Top Photo: Elmer Noeth in Stan Smith's V8-60 at Lake Hill Speedway, Missouri. August 12, 1948.

Left: Billy Humphries in the Snook Offy.

Chassis 272

duplicate #

This is another chassis numbered 272. This famous A.R.D.C. veteran with the unusual acrylic bubble trailer was owned by Gus Mutter.

The Mutter Offy was a beautiful blue and silver leafed #7 Kurtis with an Offy engine.

Dick Shugrue bought the car in 1951 and ran it as a blue and silver #7 Offy.

Dick Gallagher purchased the car from Shugrue and put a Sesco in it.

The last owners were Jim Lowery in 1976, Mel Clark and Dick Albrecht who ran the car until the time he sold it to Tommy Caruso in 1992.

Above: Frank Simonetti in the beautiful Gus Mutter Offy.

Left: The Gus Mutter trailer was as admired as his car!

Chassis 274

Louie Ligino in Illinois owns this car. The dash tag is 0-274-48.

The history of this car and the previous owners are unknown.

Chassis 275

The yellow #7 Offy owned by Gil Morcroft was part of a two car team. The cars were driven by the likes of Al Herman, Johnnie Parsons and Jimmy Bryan.

This car was sold to Ed Lowther who numbered it #77 and eventually added flames to the yellow paint scheme. Van Johnson and Jimmy Packard were two of his most exciting and talented drivers.

The next owner, Howard Patterson, kept the wild yellow and red flamed paint scheme. It was still #77 and it was Offy powered.

Bill Smith and Mel Nelson were the next owners until the Kurtis was acquired for restoration by Spike Gillespie.

Spike sold the car to Jim Barclay who sold it back to the second owner of the car, Ed Lowther. Lowther had Bill Smith restore it to his racing colors.

Ed Lowther passed away in July of 1999 and his cars were being sold in National Speed Sport News.

Top Left: Van Johnson was never really that comfortable on pavement. Here he tried to get the hang of the West 16th Street asphalt.

Top Right: Billy Mehner in the Patterson Offy.

Right: Likeable Gene Hartley in Gil Morcroft's midget at Williams Grove.

Chassis 276

Mel Owens Offy was a very recognizable white, black and red #33 Midwestern midget.

The car was driven by Don Branson, Les Scott, Arnie Knepper, Russ Congdon, Al "Cotton" Farmer, Johnny White and Jim Hemmings.

Mel Owens sold the car to Johnny Pawl and Pawl sold it to Badger driver, "Chief" Harry Whitehorse, who put a Falcon in it.

After Whitehorse's death in 1966 the car was sold to Eldon Hearn in R.M.M.R.A.

The car passed through the hands of Bob Marshall who ran it as a cream and red #6.

The last owners of the car were Mike Benjamin and Darrell Jackson before Al Craig got the chassis in 1986 as a restoration project.

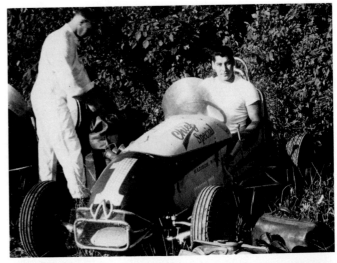

Above: "Chief" Harry Whitehorse in the former Owens car.

Below: Al "Cotton" Farmer in the Mel Owens Offy at Soldier Field.

Chassis 277

Below: Owner "Monk" Tadlock poses with driver Steve McGrath.

A.R.D.C. car owner John "Monk" Tadlock of Norfolk, Virginia was the original owner of this rather plain looking, red #8 Offy. Vernon Land and Charlie Miller were two of his drivers.

The car is probably best remembered for Charlie Miller's horrifying accident at Langhorne when Miller left the track and crashed into the trees.

Tadlock sold the car to Ed Tiella in Connecticut who had Bobby Boone and Steve McGrath as drivers.

Tiella conveyed ownership to Frank Fahey from the same state. Fahey sold the car to Jim Bardaz who never ran it in competition.

Jim Staats owned the car in 1982.

Chassis 279

I was contacted several years ago by Tom Baumgarner who informed me he had purchased a K.K. midget at an auction in Scottsdale, Arizona. The I.D. tag was 0-279-48.

Tom did not know anything about the car and he did not supply me with the names of any previous owners.

Chassis 281

The current owner, Gene Angelillo notified me that he had purchased a car with the dash tag 0-281-48.

Gene believed Richard Burgess in Connecticut ran this car as a yellow #15 in the 1960s.

Gene Angelillo still owns the car (1999).

Chassis 282

This unusual, polished aluminum car, remained unpainted.

It was sold to Henry Conrad in 1948 and it appears it was never raced.

Junior Dreyer bought the car from Conrad and sold it to Arlen Kurtis who bought the car for display purposes but decided to run it in vintage meets.

Chassis 285

Jim Staats, the current owner, sent me some great information on 0-285-48.

Latelle Miller was the initial owner. It was a beautiful red and gold #1 Offy driven by Johnny Rice and Charlie Ethier.

Jim Miller was the second owner before selling the car to Paul Young.

Young sold the Kurtis to Bill Denks. Denks transferred ownership to Gene Ciabitari.

The car was painted blue and white #52 with an Offy engine.

On August 29, 1969 A.R.D.C.'s Larry Rice was fatally injured in the car at Islip, New York.

Gene lost interest in racing and sold it to long time A.R.D.C. car owner, Tommy Smart. Tommy sold the aging Kurtis to Staats as a restoration project at the end of its racing career. Jim restored the car in the original Latelle Miller colors.

Above: Johnny Rice in the new Latelle Miller Offy.

Below: Nick Fornoro in Paul Young's Offy.

Chassis 286

Hud Meyer researched this former Frank Curtis car built in 1948.

The #8 car was painted red with white scallops, the opposite of the normal Curtis paint scheme.

It is believed that the next owner was Charlie Krick who owned it between 1949 and 1953.

Jack Yesitis from Hastings, Michigan was the next owner before selling the #87 Offy to Frank Lesko.

Lesko ran the car as a #87 Offy with the same odd scallops on the nose.

The car was believed to have been sold to "Pop" Burns in Huntington, West Virginia.

Friends of Whitey Grice remember picking up the car for Whitey Grice on August 24, 1958. Grice paid $2,450.00 for the car.

The car was painted red and gold #29 with Offy power.

Probably the most memorable owner of the car was, fashion model, Lori Rossi who owned the car from 1959 until 1962. The red #29 car was named the "Lori-B" Offy.

Lori sold the car to Dick and Owen Kincaid. The red #8 Offy was named the "Kincaid Barber Shop Special".

In 1964 the car was sold to Jack Gouldie of Racine, Wisconsin. It went through the hands of John Hancock, Barnie Barns, Jimmy Burns and Spike Gillespie before reaching the current owner, Brian Johnson.

Brian had Bob Willey do the restoration work on the car.

Left: Car owner Frank Curtis (left) and driver Henry Renard push Frank's new car out of his garage in Lynbrook, New York.

Below: Billy Compton in the "Pop" Burns car at Freeport, Long Island in 1952.

Top Right: The completed Curtis Offy with Steve McGrath behind the wheel.

Bottom Right: Ernie McCoy in the red and gold "Lori-B" Offy.

Chassis 287

Dave White, in Ohio, owns this historically important car that he believes started out as Gil Morcroft's yellow #17 Offy before being sold to Lloyd Hamm.

The Hamm Car was a very successful working K.K., unfortunately Clark "Shorty" Templeman lost his life in the car.

The midget was sold to Bob Rice who ran it as the famous #10 named, "Old Blue". The car was driven by his son, Larry Rice, before it came into the possession of the current owner,

Mr. White has restored it as the red #10 Hamm Offy.

Larry Rice poses next to "Old Blue".

Little Sonny Ates in Lloyd Hamm's Offy. Notice the identical front pusher in the Rice and Hamm car.

Dave White's restored Hamm Offy.

Chassis 293

Another acquisition of Stan Lobitz. Stan believes this car was originally Vince Caccia's car before being sold to Wayne Doerstler. He believes the next owner was Leigh Earnshaw before he bought the car.

Chassis 294

Don Black bought this car in 1989 and he felt the original owner was Paul Krueger. Subsequent owners were Gary Maier, Don Conrad and Allan Knepper.

Chassis 300

I believe Ralph Day sold this chassis to Dennis Aase in Southern California.

From Dennis it went to Bill Logan, presumably for restoration purposes.

The racing history and previous owners of this car are unknown.

Chassis 302

This car, possessing dash tag number 0-302-48, is currently owned by John Berkey.

Danny Frye allegedly told the current owner this was a local car that was painted white and yellow and sponsored by Bardahl.

The current owner, John Berkey, believes the car to be one of the Gus Sohm Cars.

Mr. Berkey did not relate who the previous owners were before he bought it for a restoration project.

Chassis 307

This is a car that August Hoffman is currently restoring as a replica of his famous black and silver #7 "Park Lumber Special" that he campaigned in the mid-fifties.

I have not been able to ascertain if this in fact is the original car.

This 1955 Photo shows Eddie Sachs dueling with Georgie Fonder at The West 16th Street Speedway in August Hoffman's #7.

Chassis 310

This first person, known to have owned this car, was John Schmick from Kansas City, Missouri.

Schmick moved to San Diego and ran the car in U.R.A. from 1953 to 1959 powered by a Ferguson tractor engine. He sold the car to Lloyd Turner.

While in the ownership of Turner, the car carried the #22 and was powered by a V-6 Buick. Martin Hagopian bought the car in the 1980s for restoration, but sold it instead to Marvin Silva.

Marvin sold the car to Bob Silva of Sacramento in April of 1998.

Interestingly the car has Offy engine #63 which was purported to have been originally owned by Fred Friday in 1940.

Top Photo: Lloyd Corbin in the Schmick #74 car.

Below: The Schmick car when Marvin Silva owned it.

Chassis 312

Len Thrall bought this car from a promoter in the Midwest that owned a three car team, numbers 31, 32 and 33.

This K.K. was the #32 car. It had an "M" in the front pusher. I saw the car run at Freeport, New York in 1956. It was an orange and white #9 Offy.

In 1965 Charles Gardner ran it in N.E.M.A. as a red #24 Offy.

The name of the next owner is unknown, however the car was called the "Ell-Bee" Offy.

After that it was owned by a man named Lane who replaced the Offy with a Chevy II.

Ralph Paradis in New Hampshire bought it as a restoration car and sold it to Tom Fitzgerald in 1995.

Len Thrall at Freeport, Long Island in 1956.

Chassis 315

This was the orange #7 Offy owned by John Wills and sponsored by Hoover Motor Express.

The car currently resides in Missouri in the possession of Charles Hornbrook.

The Offy engine is #225 (1998).

Dick Northam in John Wills orange #7 Offy, sponsored by Hoover Motor Express.

Chassis 316

John Howard in Pennsylvania bought this, his second K.K., from Robert Jacobson in New York.

Previous owners of the car and detail of the car's racing history were not available.

Chassis 318

This car, with dash tag F-318-48 was owned by Paul Waterman in 1982.

At the time Mr. Waterman knew nothing about the car's history.

Chassis 319

Another car with little more information than a dash tag was this one, owned by Jon Holcombe in 1982. The dash tag is 0-319-48.

Chassis 320

Vic Yerardi owns this car, dash tag F-320-48. No history is known.

Chassis 321

Malcolm Church from Australia informed me that he had purchased the former yellow and black #1 Dick Hennessey Offy (engine #175) driven by Bobby Albert, Gig Stephens and Bert Brooks.

Chassis 325

duplicate #

Ralph Day sold this car to a fellow named Frank Sower. Nothing is known about the car.

Chassis 325

duplicate #

The current owner, Jerry Duggan feels that this car was the Lafe Roush Chevy II.

Another car, chassis 353, is also thought to be the Roush Chevy II.

Chassis 326

Originally owned by Gays Biro, this car was sold sometime in 1954.

Dick Stuart in Florida owned it in the early 1980s. He sold it to Jerry Duggan in 1982.

Leonard "Gig" Stephens in Dick Hennessey's yellow and black Offy at Flemington, New Jersey.

Chassis 327

This famous K.K. was first owned by Moe Goff. John Pestana purchased it and painted it blue, white and red #3. It was driven by B.C.R.A. great, Dick Atkins.

The car was sold to Jerry O'Connell, sponsored by "Shamrock Truck Lines". Another midget great, and multiple B.C.R.A. Champion, Hank Butcher piloted the car.

Bobby Morrow bought the car in his rookie season and painted it canary yellow and white and elected to keep the Offy.

After its career ended, John Mosekian bought the car in 1986 and painstakingly restored it in the Pestana colors.

John Mosekian still owned the car in 1999.

Top Right Photo: Dee Hileman in the Moe Goff #3 Offy.

Bottom Left Photo: Dick Atkins in the John Pestana Offy.

Top Left Photo: Hank Butcher in Jerry OConnell's "Shamrock Truck Lines" Offy.

Lower Right Photo: Bobby Morrow in the former Goff Offy.

Chassis 329

This might be the most famous, and identifiable car that ever ran in B.C.R.A.

A 1948 K.K. owned by the legendary, George Bignotti.

Bignotti painted this little V8-60 pale blue and white sponsored by "Burgermeister Beer".

The car was driven by the brightest stars in B.C.R.A.

Bignotti sold the car to Vic Gotelli who ran it with the same colors and number.

Murph Maffei was the next owner before selling to Mike Mosekian. Mike told me the frame had seen better days!

The car was sold to Jimmy Soares in 1984 who intended to restore it.

Jimmy still owns the car (1999).

Johnny Soares in the Bignotti V8-60 in 1950,

Chassis 330

Stan Lobitz located another K.K. owned by Frank Curtis.

This car started out as a cream and red #8 built in 1948. It was sold to Georgie Rice. Interestingly, it was the only midget Rice ever owned.

Rice ran it as a cream and red #8 Offy before selling it to Avery Lampere.

Lampere campaigned the Offy as a #16. Harry Hull bought this midget and painted it his familiar purple and white #16.

He removed the Offy and installed a twin fire V8-60. The next owner was George Landry. I remember seeing Landry tool this potent V8-60 around Freeport Stadium in the late 50s.

The car was sold to Jack Hicksbeech who ran it as a Chevy II.

Stan Lobitz bought the car from Hicksbeech.

George Landry in the Harry Hull "Twin Fire" at Danbury, Connecticut.

Chassis 332

Walt Land campaigned this maroon V8-60 with the unlikely #999 in B.C.R.A.

The next owner was Norm Rapp who ran it as a yellow and red #16 V8-60.

Norm sold the car to Harvey Lord, who in turn sold it to Oregonian, Jack Corley in 1995.

Below: Norm Rapp in the former Walt Land V8-60 in 1951.
J.C. Collection

Wayne McClintock in Walt Land's #999 V8-60 in 1949.
J.C. Collection

Chassis 333

Ray Stacey, the owner of this chassis, stated that he knows nothing about the cars racing history or prior ownership.

Chassis 336

Originally owned by John Snyder of Portland, Oregon.

This 1948 K.K. was a black #77 called the "Schatz Offy". Russ Congdon was one of its drivers.

It was sold in the early 1950s to Claude Lathrop of Puyallup, Washington who ran it with W.M.R.A. and A.A.A. as the "Clear Creek Trout Farm" Offy until 1957.

In 1966 it was sold to Sid Carr but the car was never raced again.

When Sid Carr died the car was sold to Bill Cammarano, who in turn sold it to Harry Stryker.

Harry elected to paint the car like the midget he campaigned in B.C.R.A. in the 1970s, a black, red and white #99 Offy, rather than restoring it to the original Snyder paint scheme.

Russ Congdon in the Snyder #77 Offy.

Chassis 338

This is a stretched midget, that ran in C.R.A. in the 1950 and '60s.

Ted Wyronski owned the car, sponsored by Ted's Valley Cadillac.

I remember the car as a white and metallic blue #23 Chevy V8.

Wild and woolly Sonny Pratt lost his life at Ascot in this car.

Milt Jantzen acquired the sprinter and sold it to Marvin Silva of Fresno.

Marvin said the chassis is rather cobbled (1997).

END 1948

Chapter Six

1949 Numbered Chassis

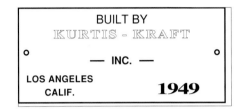

── Chapter Six ──

1949 Numbered Chassis

Chassis 341

My earliest 1949 chassis is 341 with dash tag F-341-49.

Barney Moore, the current owner of this car, has been trying to get a handle on the car's earliest owner, but so far he has been unsuccessful.

Chassis 343

The dash tag reads, 0-343-49. Larry Grimsley was the first owner of record.

The car was sold to Ray Reid and he transferred ownership to Earl Morris in 1982.

Nothing is known about the racing history of the car.

Chassis 345

duplicate

A second chassis bearing the number 345 was campaigned by Jack Rose, it ran as a #39 Offy.

The next owner was Al Rose who ran it with Offy power #32.

Smokey Secundo bought the car and ran it as a red and black #32 Offy.

The car was purchased by Joe Csiki in 1961. Its Offy engine was replaced with a Falcon six cylinder engine.

At one point Joe's car did not carry a number, instead it had a $ sign.

Joe did very well with the car winning the 1966 A.R.D.C. Championship.

The next owner was named (?) Margan, then Walt May purchased it in 1970.

It is now part of the Stan Lobitz collection.

Chassis 345

duplicate

This was originally M.A. (Marcus and Alfred) Walkers Offy.

The Walkers gave the exact date it was built, in an ad in N.S.S.N. The date of manufacture was March of 1949.

This car was their white and red #16 car that Cecil Green drove. The car was sold to Bill Meers of Oklahoma City in 1950.

This chassis, or chassis #150-the 2nd Walker Offy, was stretched into a sprinter by Buzz Barton for Bill Meers in 1951.

Jimmy Reece in the "Orchid Cleaners" sponsored Bill Meers Offy. Formerly owned by M.A. Walker. J.C. Collection

◄

Jerry Russo in Smokey Secundo's Offy

Chassis 347

This was one of the prettiest and fastest Offy midgets in the Eastern midget wars!

Bruce Homeyer owned this sanitary yellow and black #19 Offy chauffeured by the great Bobby Marshman.

Pat Ryan bought the car in 1949 and owned it until 1958. He sold the car to Ken Hickey for $1,400.00.

Hickey painted it yellow and black and sold it to a man named Pariot in St. Louis. He never raced the car.

Hickey heard that Homeyer was looking for a car so he bought the car back from Pariot for Homeyer.

In the very first outing Marshman won the Trenton "300". Bobby also won a 250 miler and several 100 milers at Trenton.

In 1963 Hickey acquired the car and he sold it to Jerry Willets.

Willets had Hank Williams and Bert Brooks drive the car.

Bottom Photo: Walt Fair in Pat Ryan's Offy.

The Offy went through the hands of Vinnie Parise, Charlie Nagy, Jim Travers and Ralph Evachuk who sold it to Spike Gillespie who restored it as the Konstant Hot #19 in 1986.

Spike sold the immaculate restoration to Kurt Ritthaler in the early 1990s.

Tony Romit was another "stand on the gas" Eastern midget driver who drove the Bruce Homeyer car.

Chassis 349

Aldo Bigioni in Ontario, Canada is the current owner of this car.

The I.D. tag is F-349-49. The history of the car is unknown.

▶

Right: Aldo Bigioni's red #21 V8-60.

Chassis 351

In 1987 Max Brattain bought F-351-49 from a broker named Jerry Harris in Decatur, Illinois.

Harris told him the K.K. belonged to Eddie Moore in St. Louis, Missouri who ran it as a #3 Chevy II.

Below: Loague Yount in the Eddie Moore Chevy II from St. Louis, Missouri.

Chassis 353

This car is currently owned (1999) by Grant Marceau from Rhode Island.

Grant traced the car back to its first known owner, Bud Simmons of "Reliable Welding" in Maywood, Illinois.

He ran the car as a #55 V8-60 in 1955. Henry Pens was one of his drivers.

The next owner was Frank Tycic from Joliet, Illinois; Adler Urbancic, aka, "Tony" Adler also from Joliet bought the car from Tycic.

Adler sold the car to Dick Pole and Gus Carlson from Glenwood, Illinois in 1967 and they ran the car as a #29 Chevy II.

Dick Pole sold out to Gus Carlson, owner of "Calumet Tool". The car was an attractive white and orange #21 with a Charley Peck nose. Jim Jeffries was the driver.

Harry Dildon was the next owner before selling the car to Carl Sandy of Lafayette, Indiana.

Sandy ran the car as a #16. Lafe Roush bought the car from Sandy and ran it as a #36 Chevy II in 1976.

Below: The "Reliable Welding" shop in Hinsdale, Illinois (1953).

Chassis 355

Brooks Carroll was the original owner of this car.

He didn't run the car often because he worked on a luxury ocean liner.

His drivers were, Russ Klar and Ed "Dutch" Schaefer.

"Dutch" bought the car and sold it to Carl Miller's son, Midge.

Miller put an Offy in the chassis. Midge ran the Offy until he blew the engine and installed an aluminum block V8.

In 1980 Miller stripped the car for parts and bought another car, he sold the chassis, less the body, to Jim Staats.

Chassis 358

Chassis F-358-49 was a pretty #55 Offy owned by Leon Mensing.

I.M.C.A. star, Dick Ritchie won the I.M.C.A. midget championship in the car.

The car was piloted by the likes of Johnny Rutherford, Bobby Marshman and Mel Kenyon.

Chassis 362
duplicate

George Turner in New York is the present owner of this chassis.

George believes this was one of the Householder K.K.s.

This red and white #55 Householder Offy was sold to Pete Snideman who also ran it as a #55 Offy.

Snideman sold the car to Forrest Parker who painted it red and white #12. Parker kept the Offy power.

Ed Hitze, the famed photographer and author bought the car and ran it as a #18 Offy. The car was driven by Bob McLean, Ronnie Duman, Bob Wente and Jimmy Davies.

Fred Hight secured the K.K. from Hitze. Hight put the #55 back on the car.

Dale Millen was the last owner before selling to George Turner.

Above: Ace photographer, Ed Hitze, poses with Ronnie Duman in the former Householder Offy.

Below: Gays Biro at Langhorne in the Householder Offy.

Below: Forrest Parker and Cotton Farmer at West 16th Street.

Chassis 362

duplicate #

Jack Gormley of Sacramento brought 0-362-49 out to California.

The car is original, and as such it is interesting. It is painted maroon powered by a V8-60 #69.

The car was bought from Joe Russo in New York.

Gormley ran the car in vintage races until a motorcycle accident sidelined him.

Jack sold the car in April 1997 to Jerry Koster in Elk Grove, California.

END 1949

Chapter Seven

1950-52 Numbered Chassis

BUILT BY
KURTIS - KRAFT
— INC. —
LOS ANGELES
CALIF.   19--

1950 Numbered Chassis

```
          BUILT BY
      KURTIS - KRAFT
  o                        o
           — INC. —
  LOS ANGELES
    CALIF.              1950
```

Chassis 364

The original owner of the previous K.K. was Joe Russo, this car's original owner was Eddie Russo! It would seem to be more than a coincidence that two members of the racing Russo clan bought cars separated by one chassis number.

Another interesting fact is the dash tag which proclaims this to be the first car built in 1950. It is F-364-50.

When Russo owned the car it was a maroon and gold Offy #97.

Harry Conklin in Denver bought it and ran it with an Offy.

Tom Roath was the penultimate owner. The last known owner was Jim Krenek of Denver in 1986.

Below: Car owner Eddie Russo poses with driver, Roger West, at Hales Corners, Wisconsin in 1968.

R.M.M.R.A. driver, Cal Chambers in Jim Krenek's Offy.

1951 Numbered Chassis

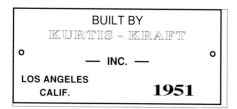

BUILT BY
KURTIS - KRAFT
— INC. —
LOS ANGELES
CALIF. **1951**

The Missing Chassis

It is interesting to note that the dash tag for Chassis #364 establishes it as a 1950 model. Chassis #365 is the only number missing between the only known 1950 Chassis and the first 1952 production.

There is no information available on the missing #365.

Below: Chuck Arnold in the Barclay Offy at Flemington (1956).

1952 Numbered Chassis

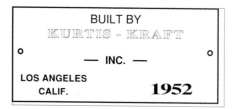

BUILT BY
KURTIS - KRAFT
— INC. —
LOS ANGELES
CALIF. **1952**

Chassis 366

The important dash tag information, 0-366-52, proclaims this car to have been built in 1952.

Ohio's Gordon McKim bought this car for his driver - Pat O'Connor.

O'Connor, never a proponent of midgets, ran the car several times at the high banked Cincinnati Bowl, garnering a 1st and 2nd place finish, before stepping out of the car.

McKim had Potsy Goacher drive for him and they won the 1952 "Night before the 500" race.

Jim Barclay bought the midget and painted it red and gold #39. It was Offy powered. Chuck Arnold was a steady driver.

The car was sold to Ken Hickey and he sold it to Bob Kline in Silver Springs, Maryland.

I believe Kline ran it as a yellow and black #63 Chevy II.

Charles Hinkle in Ohio was the last known owner (1982).

A 1981 snapshot of a very important car! The former McKim Offy.

119

Chassis 367

This car was bought new by Ken Hickey in November 1952.

Hickey painted the car black and numbered it three. He took the car to Florida for a Winter series and it won its very first race.

Ken still has the dash tag for the car, it reads, 0-367-52. Ken said he had heard that possibly one more car was built at the Kurtis plant before it was sold to Johnny Pawl, one month later.

Hickey sold the car to Sam Traylor who painted the car black #41.

Sam put Johnny Thomson and Wally Campbell in the car.

Traylor confided that Wally really wasn't cut out for midgets, he needed more horsepower to go!

Traylor later painted it red and yellow #55. This car, a personal favorite of mine, was regarded as one of the finest handling cars on the East Coast.

Traylor sold the midget to Nick Duino, a very daring young lad who's enthusiasm surpassed his ability. After only four races the young man lost his life in the car at Langhorne, Pennsylvania.

Nick's father continued to run the car for years. The next owner was Billy Meiss from Hazelton, Pennsylvania. It still carried the #55, but was powered by a Chevy II.

Donald "Brick" Taylor acquired the Kurtis from Meiss. At this point it was alleged that Eastern driver, Wayne Woodward came into possession of the car.

Stan Lobitz thinks the car is still intact and may be in the Midwest (1996).

Top: Ken Hickey's new #3 Offy, driver Len Duncan.

Middle: Johnny Thomson in the Sam Traylor Offy.

Bottom: Billy Meiss in the same car.   Arnie de Brier Photo

Chassis 888

The final chassis number in my records belongs to Erick Lieder. He said the car was built in 1949. The highest chassis number in 1949 is #363.

The only explanation for the number is that it was mismarked using an #8 die instead of the #3 die.

Mr. Lieder feels that this car was originally a maroon and white #37 Offy owned by Gus Linhares in 1957.

Harvey Guttry was the next owner in 1960. It was a red #12 powered by an Offy.

Lieder states that the last owner who ran the car competitively was John Schmick who ran it with a Fergie engine.

Erick Lieder is still the owner of the car in 1999.

Top Photo: Bud Sterrett in Gus Linhares Offy 1959.

Middle: Bob McCoy in the John Schmick Offy 1961.

Bottom: Norm Rapp in Harvey Guttry's Offy 1961.

Chapter Eight

1946 Chassis Numbers Unknown

```
        BUILT BY
    KURTIS - KRAFT
  o     — INC. —      o
 LOS ANGELES
   CALIF.        1946
```

Chapter Eight

1946 Chassis Numbers Unknown

This chapter contains the histories of 1946 Kurtis - Kraft midgets with chassis that are unknown to me, were never stamped, or were destroyed.

The chassis in this chapter, when added to the 1946 numbered chassis produces a total approximating the total 1946 Kurtis - Kraft production figures.

Johnny Balch #20 Offy

A big money winner, reputed to have won over $75,000.00 in 1946, this blue and white #20 Offy, along with Gib Lilly's V8-60 were the first K.K.'s to appear on March 17, 1946 at the L.A. Coliseum.

The car was ably driven by Eddie "The Villain" Haddad. Howard Keck bought the car at the end of the 1946 season and after campaigning it until 1949 it was stored in a warehouse.

Gene Curtis, a restorer in Southern California bought the car, but lost interest and sold the car to Lee Knox.

Knox initially painted the car black #36 with an Offy engine. Since that time Mr. Knox decided to paint it in the blue and white Balch colors. It is still in Mr. Knox's possession (1997).

Top: Eddie Haddad in the Balch Offy.

Middle: The Balch Offy at Balch's garage.   J.C. Collection

Bottom: Lee Knox restoration. Del Mar 1996.   M&M Photo.

Gib Lilly V8-60

The second K.K. to make its appearance at the L.A. Coliseum in March 17, 1946 was owned by Gib Lilly. The car was painted two tone blue #36 and it was powered by a V8-60.

Lilly never could get the quarter elliptical springs to work so he sold the car at the Gilmore "Thanksgiving Day Grand Prix" to Eddie Bourgnon for the alleged price of $12,000.00.

Bourgnon painted the car red and black #12, and replaced the V8-60 with an Offy engine.

Ted Tappett drove the car for Bourgnon but didn't care for the 1/4 elliptical spring setup anymore than Lilly had.

The car was sold to Ken Hickey, who changed the front end to a traditional transverse spring. His steady driver was Georgie Fonder.

Ken sold the car to Stan Frankenfield. Pictures of Frankenfield's white and red #2 Offy, clearly show this to be a 1946 K.K. by virtue of the rear radius rod pads and dzus button holes in the belly pans.

It is alleged that this was the car in which Tony Bonadies lost his life.

After Frankenfield's death the car was sold as part of his estate and was restored by Jim Barclay. Sadly, Barclay stated, that he cut up the original frame and replaced it with a copy!

Top Photo: Gib Lilly at Saugus 1946.   J.C. Collection

Center Photo: Ted Tappett in the red, black and gold-leafed #12 Bourgnon Offy.

Lower Photo: "Gig" Stephens in the Stan Frankenfield Offy.

Gib Lilly at the Stockton Fairgrounds, April 28, 1946.   J.C. Collection

Frank Magarian's First V8-60

Frank Magarian bought one of the first K.K. V8-60's. The car was painted white #103. Frankie Cavanaugh was one of his drivers.

After a seven year stint under the Magarian banner the car was sold in 1953 to Bill Amans and Clarance Starr who also campaigned it as a V8-60, painted red with the #3.

Glen Dennee bought the car in 1958 and owned it for nearly ten years before selling it to Sam Horton in 1967.

Sam ran it as a red and white #94 Chevy II. Sam's driver was Bud Reibhoff.

Horton sold the car to Jerry Jones in Texas. Jones was killed in a midget accident, (in another car), and the K.K. was sold to Jack Bouslog of LaPorte, Texas in 1985.

Top: Glen Dennee in his own car.　　J.M. Collection

Center: Gil Alcala in Sam Hortons car.　　J.M. Collection

Bottom: Frankie Cavanaugh in Magarian #103.

Leland "Buzz" Lowe's First V8-60

Leland Lowe's first K.K. was driven by Jack Diaz and Danny Oakes.

The black and white #124 debuted in July of 1946.

Lowe owned the car for a few short months before selling it to Frank Armi for $4,000.00!

Armi painted the car orchid and white #97. The car was sponsored by "Hanford Auto Parts".

Armi ran the midget for years before Al Hendrix sold it for him.

Hendrix could not remember to whom he sold the car.

Above: Frank Armi in his familiar #97 V8-60 formerly owned by "Buzz" Lowe.

Below: "Buzz" Lowe's car at Balboa in 1946. The driver is unknown.

Bill Krech's First Offy

Bill Krech's bronze and cream #76 Offy debuted on June 20, 1946. Dapper Dennis "Duke" Nalon was his driver.

At the end of the 1946 season the K.K. and Krech's rail frame midget, built by Willie Utzman, was sold to Herman Clevell of Natick, Massachusetts.

Clevell ran the Kurtis as a white #6 Offy. Clevell's driver, Johnny Black was the third owner of the car before selling it to Blackie La Maccia.

La Maccia sold the car to a man named Case who sold it to driver, Ronnie Evans.

Evans transferred ownership to Mario Lerardi. The car ran as a black #75 V8-60 called "Gigi's" Ford.

Stan Lobitz checked the car out thoroughly after he bought it from Lerardi and found absolutely no evidence of a chassis number.

He found weld marks where the quarter elliptical spring perches were located and the car still employed the use of 1/4" x 28 hex screws to hold the aluminum panels in place, instead of dzus buttons, this is only found on the earliest cars.

Dennis "Duke" Nalon in the first Krech K.K. at the Coliseum 1946.

Johnny Black in Herman Clevell's Offy. Black became the third owner of the car. Note the quarter elliptical springs denoting it as one of the earliest cars built at Kurtis - Kraft.

Edelbrock V8-60

The orange and red #63 Edelbrock V8-60 that appeared of June 19, 1946 became known as the "Offy Killer" when its driver, Rodger Ward, defeated a field of snarling Offies at Gilmore in 1949.

The genius behind the car was a legend in the field of high performance automotive engineering, Vic Edelbrock.

Edelbrock sold his midget to Midwestern car owner, Frank Pavese.

It is rare when a race car achieves legendary status during its racing life as this car did!

Every subsequent owner of this car ran it in the white and blue Edelbrock colors, #27 with Ford V8-60 power.

Pavese had some well known Midwestern drivers including, Bud Hoppe, Willie Wildhaber and Bob Tattersall, who made the car famous in the Midwest, especially on the day he beat the Offies badly at Terre Haute.

When Frank Pavese became gravely ill he sold the car to Danny Frye.

The car was painted white and blue #27 with the V8-60. It was Danny Frye Jr.'s first midget ride.

Frye later sold the aging K.K. to Mike Riley. Riley ran the car for a while before retiring the badly rusted, aged, warhorse.

The Edelbrock family learned of the existence of the car and offered Riley a reported sum of between $22,000.00 and $25,000.00 for it.

I am told the car has been restored and it resides in the entrance of the Edelbrock company.

Top Photo: Danny Frye Jr. got his first ride in his father's car, the ex - Pavese V8-60.

Lower Photo: Bob Tattersall in the Pavese "Twin Fire V8-60" at Terre Haute.

Rex Mays #44 Offy

Rex Mays' white, black and red #44 Offy was driven by racing greats like, Mel Hansen, Duke Nalon and Joe Garson.

While it is true Mays didn't care for driving midgets, he was shrewd enough to realize that a midget, properly run could be a lucrative investment.

After Mays' death in 1949, the midget was sold to Al Willey.

Al painted the Offy red and silver #44. Johnny Hobel was his driver.

The car was sold to Henry Hargrove who sold it to Hugh McCullough after running the car for a brief period.

Hugh McCullough was the last owner to campaign the #44 "Dairy Queen" sponsored car.

In September of 1952 the car was ripped in half in a horrifying crash on the backstretch at the DuQuoin, Illinois mile.

The driver, Buddy Cagle, was lucky to have only received a concussion in the accident.

Top Photo: One of the most unusual photos of the Edelbrock V8-60. Eastern midget great, Bill Schindler, visiting California for "Turkey Night" in 1946, tried out the cockpit of the Edelbrock car at Balboa.

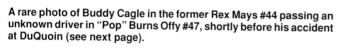

A rare photo of Buddy Cagle in the former Rex Mays #44 passing an unknown driver in "Pop" Burns Offy #47, shortly before his accident at DuQuoin (see next page).

The three photo sequence clearly evidences the fact the the former Rex Mays car was completely destroyed in the 1952 DuQuoin crash!

Below: "Bullet" Joe Garson in the Rex Mays Offy at Soldier Field in Chicago.

Manuel Pontes V8-60

On July 19, 1946 B.C.R.A. member, Manuel Pontes, unveiled his new #44 red V8-60 with Buck Whitmer at the wheel.

Manuel Pontes is an obscure figure about whom little or nothing is known.

Johnny Soares and Lenny Gonsel thought he might have belonged to a Bay Area Hot Rod club.

Pontes sold his car to Carl Hahn who ran the car as a #2 V8-60.

The car passed through the hands of Amans & Starr, George Tamblyn, Lloyd Ridge and Dick Geide before Chuck Robins put a Chevy II in the blue and orange #33 K.K.

Richie Garcia bought the car from Chuck Robins and sold it to the last owner, Tony Karis in 1983.

Top Photo: Bill Amens in the Amens and Starr V8-60. J.M. Collection

Middle Photo: Gary Johnson in Chuck Robins car in 1966.
J.M. Collection

Buck Whitmer in the Manuel Pontes V8-60. Pontes became the first owner of a K.K. in B.C.R.A. J.C. Collection

The First Lutes/Gdula Offy

One of the earliest K.K. midgets to find its way to the Midwest was owned by Eddie Gdula, (pronounced Guh-doo-lah).

The earliest pictures of the car show George Witzman in the unpainted, un-numbered car at Langhorne on October 12, 1946.

Gdula sold the car to Frank Bardazon who ran it as a red #5 Offy in the 1960s.

Current status of the chassis is unknown, however it is thought to have been acquired by "Booby" Logan.

Jimmie James #28 Offy

Jimmie James fielded an awesome three car team.

His earliest K.K. was the maroon and cream #28 car, driven by Johnny McDowell, Johnnie Parsons and Aaron Woodward.

The car made its first appearance in November of 1946. The car was sold to Johnny Stenderup in 1949.

Stenderup ran it as a white and red #43 Offy. Subsequent owners and its current location are unknown.

Top Photo: George Witzman in the Lutes/Gdula Offy at Langhorne, October 12, 1946.

Bottom Photo: Tommy Copp in the Frank Bardazon Offy. The legend, "Lutes Offy" is still visible on the hood.

Top Photo: Johnny Stenderup in the former Jimmie James car.
J.C. Collection

Bottom Photo: Aaron Woodard in the #28 Jimmie James Offy.

Bert Faymonville V8-60

Bert Faymonville's red and white #85 V8-60 debuted in November of 1946 with Jack Diaz in the saddle.

Early pictures of the car depict anything but a high dollar operation!

In the early 1950s Faymonville sold the car to Willie Swift.

The car passed through the hands of Willie Swift, Joe Binter, Jerry Richardson, Barry Knowlton and Steve Searock, before being acquired by Steve Stapp.

When Stapp got the car it was transformed into a pretty red #88 Offy.

Steve ran in U.S.A.C. and B.C.R.A. taking turns behind the wheel with B.C.R.A. regular, Gene Gurney.

The car made its way to Northern California when George Benson took over ownership of the car.

George sold it to his friend and car owner, Ollie Johnson.

Ollie sold the car to another Santa Clara Valley resident, Floyd Alvis.

Alvis put a Chevy II engine in the blue, silver and black #73.

Floyd sold the car to Larry Welch who campaigned the K.K. as a blue #73. Welch was the last owner of record.

If this chassis ever turns up it is sure to be stamped with a low number.

Top Photo: Jack Diaz in the Bert Faymonville V8-60.

Middle Photo: Gene Gurney in Steve Stapp's Offy 1960.

Bottom Photo: B.C.R.A. Champion Floyd Alvis in the former Bert Faymonville car.
J.M. Collection

Ken Smith V8-60

Ken Smith bought this "kit car" in 1946 and put the red and gold #147 V8-60 together in early 1947.

Smith sold the Kurtis to Ray Wiley who painted it maroon and copper #10 with a V8-60 engine.

Wiley had Johnny Baldwin and Dickie Reese as his drivers.

Ray sold the car to Guido Ginochio in 1948. In the mid 50s Guido painted the car in gold metalflake.

Guido kept the car until 1955 when he sold it to Jack Williams.

Williams only kept the car a year before selling it to Jim Correia in 1956. Correia ran it as a white #25 and a red #98 V8-60.

After 1960 the car disappeared.

Top: Johnny Baldwin in the Ray Wiley V8-60.

Bottom: Dickie Reese in Guido Ginochio's heavily metalflaked car.

Vince Podrugiel Drake

Wild Bill Zaring and Cliff Epp made this little red #64 Drake fly!

In 1949 the car carried a distinctive checkerboard paint job.

Robert Henley purchased the car in 1951 and ran it as a blue, red and white #33 Drake sponsored by "Maywood Ford".

The present owner of the car is unknown.

Vince Podrugiel's Drake with "Wild" Bill Zaring in the cockpit.

Fred Gerhardt Drake

In 1946 this was a dark maroon and white #39 Drake driven in U.R.A. by Johnnie Parsons and Billy Cantrell.

Billy Cantrell became a part owner in the car in 1947. The car was painted red and white #16.

In 1949 Jack Taylor bought the car and ran it as a blue #28 Fergie.

Taylor is the last registered owner in 1950.

Right: Johnny Baldwin in the Bill Cantrell Drake.

Marv Edwards First K.K.

Marv Edwards first K.K. was a red and black #60 purchased in 1946. Frank "Satan" Brewer was his first driver.

The car was the only early Kurtis - Kraft that I have found that employed the use of quarter elliptical springs, front and rear!

Doug Grove drove the car in the early 1950s and it was getting pretty rough looking.

Marv refurbished the car, painted it white and red #54 and sold it in Australia in 1959.

According to my correspondents the car has been restored.

Top: Frank "Satan" Brewer in the Marv Edwards Offy as it appeared in 1947. J.C. Collection

Left: Doug Grove in the well seasoned Marv Edwards Offy!

McDowell/Balch #33 Offy

The black and white #33 Offy driven by Johnny McDowell was sold to Hart Fullerton in October of 1947.

One theory holds that Hart Fullerton sold the K.K. to a man named Bob Edwards in Indiana.

Edwards ran the car in Southern Indiana and Kentucky with Jimmy Zollman as his chauffeur.

Danny Frye thought this car might have been involved in an on-track incident in Indiana when a boy was killed or badly injured running across the track.

This story is unsubstantiated, but if correct, it might hold a clue to the current disposition of the car.

Below: Johnny McDowell in the Balch/McDowell Offy in 1946.
J.C. Collection

Ernie Casale #25 Offy

This car started out as a blue and white #25 Offy midget driven by Sam Hanks in its maiden race on December 8, 1946.

Johnny Mantz was Casale's steady driver. Competing mostly in Southern California, but on one occasion he took the car to Langhorne, Pennsylvania for the legendary 100 miler in 1947.

Casale sold the car to Frankie Cal when the midgets went bust and it was stretched into a sprint car.

Racing historian, Marty Himes is the current owner of the red and white #52 Offy.

Rex Records blasts off the corner at the Reading Fairgrounds in the Frankie Cal Offy sprinter - the former Casale #25.

Below: Johnny Mantz in the Ernie Casale midget as it appeared in 1947.   **J.C. Collection**

Howard Lux Offy

This is a very obscure automobile. The car seems to have been predominantly raced on asphalt in Southern California.

The car was a red #59 Offy driven almost exclusively by "Monopoly" Mack Hellings.

In 1947 the car virtually disappeared. Racing historians have been trying to locate it for years.

Right: Mack Hellings in the Howard Lux Offy at the Coliseum in 1946.

Perry Grimm # 65 V8-60

Perry Grimm seems to be one of the people who rarely drove this car!

While Perry was driving the potent Edelbrock car he employed drivers like Rodger Ward and Gib Lilly to run his car.

The current location of this car is obscured by the fact that Perry took the car to Australia and may have sold it there.

Right Photo: Gib Lilly kept Perry Grimm's car in the winners circle at U.R.A. Red Circuit midget races.

Bottom Photo: A great shot of Gib Lilly in Perry Grimm's car.

Johnny Goss V8-60

This car was one of the 1946 Kurtis - Kraft's that found its was to the Pacific Northwest.

Goss ran it in Southern California and in Oregon and Washington.

After Johnny Goss was killed, flagging a race, the car disappeared.

Right: Sam Hanks in the Johnny Goss #93 at Balboa in 1946.

Bill Krech #90 Offy

This car started out as an unpainted #90 in November of 1946.

It was #5 in 1947 and the familiar #76 in 1948.

This could be the car that was later sold to Jim Gary driven by Johnnie Tolan.

Right: "Gentleman" Jack McGrath in the Bill Krech Offy at Soldier Field in Chicago on a chilly spring day in 1948. Notice the quarter elliptical springs.

Roscoe Hogan #34

I spoke to Roscoe Hogan in 1995 and he told me that he bought this car as a kit in 1946.

Roscoe's white and red #34 was normally driven by Norm Holtkamp.

Bob Barkhimer said it was the finest handling Kurtis - Kraft midget he had ever driven!

The disposition of this car is unknown.

Right: Norm Holtkamp in the Roscoe Hogan car. Not the best looking car but a great handling K.K. J.C. Collection

141

Ed Davis & "Lefty" Dressen #37 Offy

The Ed Davis and "Lefty" Dressen Offy was driven by Johnny Mantz and Karl Young in Southern California.

In 1947 Dressen took the car back to the Midwest and ran it at Walsh Stadium with Eastern midget ace Ernie Gesell as his driver.

I possess a photo of the Davis & Dressen car painted yellow with the #17. I can only assume the car was sold in St. Louis, Missouri.

The Davis and Dressen car in the Midwest, the owner and driver are unknown.

"King" Karl Young in the Ed Davis and "Lefty" Dressen Offy in 1946.

Arnold Krause Offy

The last car I have in my records for 1946 is the Arnold Krause Offy that first appeared as an unpainted #77.

The car was listed in the possession of Arnold Krause until 1949. The whereabouts of this car is a mystery.

Walt "Little Dynamo" Faulkner in the Arnold Krause Offy in 1948.

143

Chapter Nine

1947 - 1952 Chassis Numbers Unknown

```
BUILT BY
KURTIS - KRAFT
— INC. —
LOS ANGELES
CALIF.              19--
```

—— Chapter Nine ——

1947 -1952 Chassis Numbers Unknown

This chapter contains the histories of K.K. midgets that were built between 1947 and 1952.

No attempt has been made to sort this list chronologically. A 1949 chassis might precede a 1947 chassis etc.

Lee Grismer Offy

Lee Grismer's yellow and blue Offy was a potent iron on Southern California speedways.

Grismer sold the K.K. to Ray Vannaman who also ran it as a yellow and blue Offy.

Ken Smith bought the car and painted it tan and white #21 with Offy and V8-60 power.

One of the most memorable pictures of the Smith car depicts it flipping wildly at Fresno's Kearney Bowl in 1955 with Earl Motter's hapless form hanging out the car.

Smith sold the midget in 1959 to Sam Crull and Floyd Glidewell. The next owner, Floyd Hughes acquired the car and painted it red and white #21 with V8-60 power, later replacing the V8-60 with a Falcon.

Veterans Johnny Baldwin and Tommy Morrow drove for him.

Hughes sold the car to Midwestern car owner, Lou Cooper at the Thanksgiving Grand Prix in 1964.

It appears that Cooper immediately transferred ownership to Bill Kollman.

Kollman put U.A.R.A. champ Russ Sweedler in the car until a devastating accident nearly took his life in April of 1965.

The racing scribes of the time say it took Kollman four months to get the car back in action in August of 1965!

The question remains, was this the same chassis?

Legend has always held that the car was destroyed in a bad crash about six months after the car was purchased.

This recently discovered information suggests that the chassis may be intact.

Top: Bob Barker in the Lee Grismer Offy at Gilmore 1949.

Bottom: Russ Sweedler in the Bill Kollman car 1965.

145

Lloyd Axel #55 Offy

Leroy Byers informed me that this car ran as a team car to Lloyd Axel's #5 Offy.

This car was sometimes driven by Bert McNeese and Earl Kouba.

Lloyd sold it in Southern California to Hal Robb and it became the famous brown #55 car that Robb dubbed, "The Jewel".

After years of running the car, Robb sold it to Mickey Thompson.

Thompson wedged a Buick V-6 in the chassis as an experiment. Jim Hurtubise took some turns at the wheel but this car never ran reliably.

Danny Frye believes the car was brought to the Midwest and sold to Loague "Deputy Dawg" Yount who ran it as a red #4 Chevy II.

Jim Chini felt the chassis was cut up and disposed of by Mickey Thompson.

Above: Frank Armi in Hal Robb's "Jewel".

Below: Bert McNeese in Lloyd Axel's Offy.

Miles Spickler's Plaid Offy

A well known car in the Denver area was Miles Spickler's car dubbed "The Plaid Offy" because it was literally painted plaid when it was sponsored by O'Meara Ford.

The handsome little Offy driven by Roy Bowe won both the 1948 and 1949 R.M.M.R.A. championships.

Curt Stockwell acquired the car from Spickler before selling it to Jack Lee.

Jack Lee transferred ownership to Ray Swan in Southern California. Swan ran the beautiful red and white #3 Offy at W.R.A. vintage events.

Top Right: Ray Swan's restored Spickler Offy.

Below: Roy Bowe in the Miles Spickler Offy 1949.

Mike Caruso "Deuce"

Arguably one of the most famous midgets built by Kurtis - Kraft was a car Harry Stephens couldn't seem to get to work for him!

Mike Caruso and Bill Schindler went to California to get a Kurtis - Kraft after the drubbing they took at the hands of Chet Gibbons and George Rice in the Frank Curtis K.K.'s at the March opener at Deer Park, Long Island in 1947.

Harry Stephens wanted to unload his blue and yellow Offy #9, sponsored by "Delta Chem" and a deal was struck.

The car was repainted as a black, white and gold leafed #2 driven by the legendary, Bill Schindler.

Schindler won a great many of his astounding 106 main events between 1947 and 1948 in this car.

This car is legend on the East Coast.

Two views of Bill Schindler in the Caruso Offy.

Henning "Junior" Loock

Henning "Junior" Loock ran this car in U.R.A., in 1947 as a tan #185 V8-60.

Loock sold the car to Carl Bliss who ran the car as a white and blue #73.

The car moved to Northern California when it was acquired by Moe Goff. Goff ran the car as a cream color #72 V8-60 indoors and sold the car to B.C.R.A. heavyweight, Jack London.

London had Jack Hageman revamp the car's body and campaigned it in his familiar blue, red and white colors #4 with an Offy replacing the V8-60.

The car was then sold to Chuck Lawlor and Harry Stryker.

Harry bought out Lawlor and ran the car until 1966.

Bob Consani bought the car in 1967 and put Billy Vukovich in the car.

Burt Foland bought the car in 1968 and ran it as a black and red Offy in B.C.R.A.

Bob Thomas bought the pretty little K.K. from London, who had repurchased it from Foland.

Bob ran it in the London colors of blue, red and white with the #5.

Thomas took a couple of wild rides in the midget but came out of them unscathed.

Bob sold the car to Rex Bolen, the last known owner of the car.

In a recent conversation with Bob Thomas he told me he thought the car might have been sold by Bolen to someone in the Denver area (1998).

Top Photo: Carl Bliss in the former Henning Loock V8-60.

Middle Photo: Chuck Lawlor in Harry Stryker's Offy, still in London colors 1962 .
J.M. Collection

Bottom Photo: Rex Bolen in the former Stryker Offy 1973.
J.M. Collection

John Ramp Offy

Certain people are associated with a particular car. In the minds of racing people, Leroy Warriner will always be associated with the potent blue and white #67 Offy owned by John Ramp.

The immaculate little Offy with the Hillegass nose was sold to Leslie Cadwell who also ran it as a white and blue #67.

Warriner won the AAA National Championship in the car in 1953.

Bob Higman acquired the Offy in 1955 and while in his ownership it was driven by Gene Hartley, Leroy Warriner and Bob Wente. It was also driven by A.J. Foyt in 1957 and '58.

Higman sold the car to Gary Irvin, who sold it to Eric Morrison on the East Coast. The car then went to Roxana, Illinois and is now in Canada.

Top Right: A.J. Foyt in Bob Higman's Offy at Milwaukee in 1957.

Center Right: Leroy Warriner in the John Ramp Offy.

Frank Kurtis Offy

Not many people are aware of the fact that Frank Kurtis owned a tan and cream colored #24 Offy midget for a very brief period in 1947.

The car was driven by Joe Garson. Kurtis sold the car to Bill Murphy.

In 1948 Murphy painted the car red #26. In 1949 the car was a black #6 Offy that ran with A.A.A. Troy Ruttman was a steady driver. Murphy kept the car until at least 1956 when the car was registered in U.S.A.C. as a red and white #31 Offy driven by Skee Redican.

Below: Joe Garson in the ex - Frank Kurtis Offy after Bill Murphy purchased the car 1947.

Ike Baumbach V8-60

Ike Baumbach's blue and white #9 Barker powered car was sold to Lillian Miller.

Tommy Morrow was one of the drivers of the white and red #9 V8-60.

The next owner was Bill Lalonde who put in a Chevy II.

Bob Yuhre purchased the car from Lalonde and re-painted it gold and white #17 with a Chevy II engine.

I spoke to Bob Yuhre in 1999. He told me the chassis of the former Baumbach car was ready to break in two. He replaced the K.K. chassis with a Walt Reiff copy.

Above: Freddie Agabashian in Ike Baumbach's #21 Barker.

Below: Tommy Morrow in Lillian Miller's V8-60.

Carl Anderson Offy

Carl Anderson's 1947 K.K. was well known in the Midwest.

Anderson had drivers like Aaron Woodard, Ernie Gesell and Johnny Tolan pilot the attractive maroon and goldleafed #37 Offy.

In 1955 the car was sold to Ashley Wright who painted the car in its most memorable paint scheme. The car was black with a goldleafed starburst #2.

Templeman and the "Deuce" were unstoppable, winning the 1956 U.S.A.C. National and Midwest Championship.

Between 1956 and 1957 Ashley Wright had some of the greatest drivers pilot the "Deuce".

Drivers like Don Branson, Frank Burany, Lloyd Ruby, Chuck Rodee and Len Sutton.

Wright sold the car in 1958 to George Bignotti who painted it white, black and red with the Bowes Seal Fast logo on the hood of the #2 Offy.

Johnny Boyd towed the car back to California and shortly after it arrived, Sim Clark purchased the car.

Sim was never happy with the Offy, preferring stock block V8-60 and Chevy powered cars.

Clark sold the car of Ollie Johnson who painted it blue, white and red #96.

Joe Soares, Tommy Morrow, Shiner Watkin and Shorty Templeman drove for Ollie.

Johnson sold the car to Norm Britton who painted the car DayGlo red #18 with an Offy engine.

Bill Vukovich got his first midget ride in the car. George Snider and Rick Henderson were other notable drivers of the Britton "iron".

Norm parked the car in 1966. Sixteen years later, in 1982, I bought what remained of the car from Britton.

I accomplished about 75% of the restoration before selling the car to Bob Neilson in Ukiah, California. Interestingly, I never found a chassis number on the frame.

Neilson restored the car to the condition it was in when it was owned by Ashley Wright in 1956.

It is still owned by Neilson (1999).

Top Left: Shorty Templeman in Ashley's car at West 16th Street in 1956.

Center Left: Car owner, Ollie Johnson, poses with driver Shiner Watkin, seated in the former Ashley Wright "Deuce".

Lower Left: Gary Johnson in the Norm Britton Offy.

Above: Bob Neilson's restored Ashley Wright "Hardwood Door" Offy.   J.C. Photo

Right: Aaron Woodard in the Carl Anderson Offy in 1947.

George Bignotti #108

One of three cars maintained by George Bignotti in 1947 was this maroon and white #108 V8-60.

The car was sold to Jim Yamoka who painted it black #108 with V8-60 power.

Tommy Rice campaigned the car in the Denver area and it may have ended up in R.M.M.R.A.

Top photo: George Bignotti in his own #108 V8-60.

Lower photo: Tommy Rice in the Jim Yamoka's V8-60.

Rudy Tarditti Drake

This is probably best remembered as the flipping car that photographer Russ Reed caught pirouetting on its nose at the Contra Costa Speedway in Walnut Creek. The series of photos appeared in "Look" magazine.

Rudy Tarditti's Drake was painted yellow and blue #64. It was built in 1947.

Don Axtell bought the car from Tarditti and ran it from 1955 - 1958. It was painted white #18.

Bob Wilkins bought the car in 1964 and replaced the "Shaker" with a V8-60. The car was painted black with the #46.

Tommy Thompson purchased the car in 1967 and ran it as a #47 V8-60 and then he replaced the aging V8-60 with a more potent Chevy II.

Tommy resides in Alabama and still owns the car.

Top: Jack Barney in Rudy Tarditti's Drake.

Middle: Bob Wilkins in the former Tarditti car.

Bottom: Tommy Thompson in the car 1973.   J.M. Collection

Vito Calia #2 Offy

The pretty #2 car owned by the somber veteran from Kansas City, Missouri, Vito Calia was sold to Jim McVay, the father of Jimmy and Eddie McVay.

McVay purchased the car in 1960. He kept the car for less than a year before selling it to Danny Frye.

Frye told me he sold the car in Ohio. Unfortunately the name of the buyer is not known.

Right: Vito Calia in his own Offy, sponsored by the "Old Timers" bar.

#45 & #46 Litenberger Offies

The Litenberger Brothers owned two Offy midgets #45 and #46.

The #45 car was stretched into a sprint car that became a fixture in the East Coast.

The red and white #45 sprinter was driven by Jimmy Bryan, Elmer George, Georgie Fonder, Johnny Kay and Ralph Ligouri. Ligouri won a memorable "Twin 50" race at Langhorne in the car in 1957.

Former car owner and racing historian, Joe DiMaio, informed me that the #46 Litenberger midget, driven by Neal Carter was bought by Lee Wallard.

Wallard sold the car after racing it for a brief time to Burt Fleischman from Buffalo, New York.

Burt Fleischman, (aka), "Ted Jones", ran the car as a #99 Offy.

Burt sold the car to Howie Hines in Long Island.

Hines ran it as a #3 Offy. Lou Fray and Howie Marotti were two of his drivers.

The current location of the car is unknown.

Top Right: Roy Sherman in the Litenberger Offy midget.

Center Right: Neal Carter in the #46 Litenberger midget.

Bottom Right: Howie Marotti in the Howie Hines' midget. The last known owner of the car.

Top Left: 1957 Midwest Sprint Champion, Elmer George next to the Litenberger #45 stretched midget.

Bottom Left: Burt Fleischman in the former Litenberger Offy.

Walter Schmidhorst Offy

More people recognize this as the famous #32 Offy sponsored by Jo Jo's Restaurant than as the Walter Schmidhorst Offy.

Popular, Paul "Potsy" Goacher, was identified with this ride. When the car was red #35 Johnny Key drove the car.

Key lost his life in this car at Cincinnati, Ohio in 1954 when he fell out of the car and was run over by another driver.

Walter Schmidhorst sold the car to Justin King, it was painted white and black #79.

Top Right: Paul "Potsy" Goacher in the Schmidhorst Offy.

Center Right: Clark "Shorty" Templeman in Justin King's Offy.

Elmer Freeber Offy

This is another car better known in the Midwest by its sponsors name than the actual owner of the car.

This unusually painted blue and white #27 Offy was sponsored by "Marquette Tool and Die".

In 1961 Buddy Cagle journeyed East and copped a second at Langhorne in a 100 miler in the car.

Chuck Rodee gave it plenty of hard rides as well.

The car was sold to Jack Stroud who campaigned it as a #25 Offy. Danny Frye won the 1965 S.L.A.R.A. Championship in the car.

Bob Tattersall took the car to Australia and sold it there.

Buddy Cagle at Langhorne in the Elmer Freeber Offy 1961.

157

Walter Pew Offy

Understated elegance is the only way to describe this racing jewel!

The Pew Offy, campaigned in A.R.D.C. by Rex Records and Art Cross, was painted in black lacquer with a silver leafed #7 on the tail with the legend, Pew Offy in flowing script on the hood.

The elegant little Kurtis was sold to Mutt Anderson who campaigned the magnificent handling car with the same paint scheme and number as the two previous owners.

Troy Ruttman, Mike Nazaruk, Potsy Goacher, Mel McGaughy and Jimmy Davies were some of the throttle stompers who drove for him.

Anderson sold the car to Bill Weaver who in turn sold it to August Hoffman around 1955.

Gus put the effusive Eddie Sachs in the cockpit. The car, still a black #7 Offy, had "Park Lumber Special" on its hood. Sachs fit the car perfectly and with Mutt Anderson as the head wrench the combination won many races.

Mutt Anderson has restored a car that is alleged to be his old car. I have also heard that August Hoffman is restoring a car that is alleged to be his car.

Top: Mel McGaughy in Mutt Anderson's car at West 16th Street 1956.

Bottom: The very talented, Art Cross, in the Walter Pew Offy.

Jack Turner Offy

This washed out, pale blue, Offy K.K. kit car notched two A.A.A. National Championships for Turner in successive years, 1954 and 1955.

On the side of the car was the nickname, "Cactus Jack". The nickname was 180 degrees from reality. Turner was a pavement smoothie who learned the tricks of the trade on the paved tracks in the Pacific Northwest.

It was rumored that Turner sold this car to Roy Graham.

I contacted Jack and he confirmed that he had indeed sold his car to Roy Graham in Buffalo, New York.

Graham ran the car as a red #12 Offy in A.R.D.C. Graham sold the car to another A.R.D.C. car owner Bill "Pop" Guenther.

The car, called "Guenther's Growler" was also red with the #12 and Offy powered.

The current owner of the car is not known, however, it is possible that this car was sold to Fritz Meyer.

Top: Jack Turner at Gardena in 1955 in his own Offy.

Bottom: Lee Ferrington in Bill Guenther's "Growler".

Leonard Faas #16 Offy

This car was a blue, white and red #16 Offy driven by Faas and Walt Faulkner.

Leonard sold the car to Harold Guidi of Palo Alto, California.

Harold painted the car red and white with an attractive scallop pattern, not unlike the Faas signature scallop design. Emblazoned on the hood was the name of the sponsor, "Paramount Roofing". The car was #15 propelled by a potent Offy under the hood.

George Amick, Jim Hurtubise, Johnny Boyd and Johnny Baldwin were some of Guidi's "leadfoots".

George Amick annexed the 150 lap Thanksgiving Day Grand Prix at Gardena in the car in 1957.

Hurtubise tried for an altitude record at Ascot and almost ended up in the cheap seats outside of turn one! It is reported he clambered out of the car laughing after the scary incident.

The next owner was Glen Dennee. The car looked virtually the same as when Guidi owned it.

Hank Butcher took the little Offy to Australia to race and sold it to Jack Poritt at the end of the tour.

The car is still believed to be in Australia.

Top: George Amick twists the Harold Guidi Offy at Clovis in 1957.

Center: Ouch! Jim Hurtubise walked away from this one in 1961 at Ascot laughing.

Bottom: Walt Faulkner in the Leonard Faas blue, white and red Offy at Gilmore in 1948.

Eddie Meyer #58 Kurtis

Eddie Meyer's blue and white #58 was sold to B.C.R.A. owner, Ed Pippo, the nephew of Vic Gotelli, in 1947.

Pippo left the car the same colors and number in 1947. He campaigned the car until the following year.

The next owner of the car was Bill Johnson who ran it from 1948 to 1952. The car was a blue and white V8-60.

Jimmy Sills, Sr. bought the car in 1953 and numbered it #666. After a single season he sold it to Perry Scott and Chuck Booth.

Perry Scott became the sole owner of the car from 1955 until 1956.

Verne Morrison and Gino Freson bought the car from Scott and raced it from 1957 to 1958.

Jim Kinner purchased the car in 1959 and usually ran it as a black and red V8-60.

Kinner sold the car to Gerry Scarborough in 1965.

Scarborough put a Chevy II in the car and ran it with the #86.

In 1971 Jim McCune owned the car and it was painted red.

The last owner who raced the car in B.C.R.A. was Bill Lytell in 1973, it was a red and yellow #86 Chevy II.

Top Photo: Johnny Baldwin in the Ed Pippo #26 V8-60, formerly the Eddie Meyer car 1948.

Middle Photo: Jan Opperman in the Gerry Scarborough V8-60 in 1965.
                                                      J.M. Collection

Bottom Photo: Jim McCune in the former Meyer car after an extensive facelift in 1972.
                                                      J.M. Collection

Ernie Ruiz Offy

This 1948 Kurtis was revamped by Fred Glass who changed the hood, radiator shell and grille.

The car's original paint scheme was orange and white. At times it was painted blue and white.

It debuted as a #26 but the car was usually a #7.

The car had an Offy that was considered to be "tired", no more powerful than an average V8-60!

Most drivers couldn't get the car to go. Bob Veith was an exception, he definitely made the car go!

After Ruiz' ownership the car was sold to Tommy Astone, Sr. who ran it as a white #79 Offy, with son Tommy Astone, Jr. behind the wheel.

Astone sold the car to Andy Johnson who put a Volvo in the car and repainted it black, white and silver #92.

The next owners were Bob Silva, then Gary Koster who sold it to Al Burns in Texas.

The late auto racing writer, Phil LeVrier, purchased the car from Burns.

When LeVrier passed away it was bequeathed to his brother.

Top Photo: "King" Karl Young in the new Ernie Ruiz Offy at Balboa, 1948. The moustached gentleman kneeling behind the car is Ernie Ruiz.

Middle Photo: Tommy Astone in his father's car in 1969.
J.M. Collection

Bottom Photo: Rick Koster in Gary Koster's Chevy II in 1977. Koster sold the car to Al Burns in Texas.   J.M. Collection

Fred Friday V8-60

Fred Friday purchased a Kurtis that he ran in B.C.R.A. in 1948.

The V8-60 was a black and gold #3. Friday ran the car until 1950.

In 1951 he sold the car to Jim Ahearn. Ahearn sold the #9 V8-60 to Buzz Balfour in the same year.

Balfour painted it yellow and blue #9. The car was driven on occasion by the controversial leadfoot, Ed Elisian.

Balfour last ran the car in 1952. The current location of the car is unknown.

Top Photo: Fred Friday in his own V8-60 that he ran in B.C.R.A. in 1948.
J.C. Collection

Bottom Photo: A smiling Ed Elisian standing next to Buzz Balfour's car.   J.C. Collection

Mike Casale Offy

Mike Casale's red and white Offy gained notoriety as the car in which Bobby Ball was gravely injured in 1952 at Culver City.

Ball remained in a coma for more than a year before passing away.

Casale sold the car to Gus Linhares who in turn sold it to Leroy Kail.

Kail ran it as a white and red #17 Offy.

Kail hired sprint car drivers, Jim Hurtubise, Ned Spath and Bobby Hogle to pilot his car.

The car migrated to Northern California when Floyd Alvis purchased it from Kail.

Alvis pulled the Offy and installed a Chevy II in the red, white and black car.

Bob Sousa bought the car from Alvis and ran it with the Chevy II.

The last known owner of the car was Mike Valencia who disassembled it and stored the parts in his cellar (1982).

Top: Buddy Lee in Leroy Kail's Offy in 1961.

Center: Floyd Alvis in the ex - Kail Offy in 1971. J.M. Collection

Below: Bobby Ball in Mike Casale's #5 car at Balboa in 1948.

Tony Saylor V8-60

Tony Saylor had a two car team. The cars were painted yellow with brown numbers.

Midget great, Bob Tattersall drove the #55 Offy and took it to Australia.

The #57 V8-60 was sold to Nick Stropoli who ran it as a #77 yellow and brown V8-60.

The car was eventually sold to Walter Mordenti. It was a blue #78 V8-60 driven by Chet Conklin, Ronnie Evans and King Carpenter.

The current ownership of the car is not known.

Above: King Carpenter in the Walter Mordenti V8-60.

Lew Bruns Offy

A pretty little Kurtis campaigned in Southern California A.A.A. races in the early 1950s.

The legendary Jimmy Bryan, Billy Garrett and Jimmy Reece were three of the drivers who drove the yellow and red #28 Offy for Lew Bruns.

Bruns sold the potent K.K. to Doug Caruthers who put Bill Cantrell and Roger McCluskey behind the wheel of the then yellow and white #34 Offy.

In a qualifying attempt at Vallejo in 1965 Don Horvath struck a short length of telephone pole at the exit to the pits in turn three and was killed instantly.

Caruthers never raced the car again.

Billy Garrett in Lew Bruns Offy.

Johnny Pawl #19 Offy

This was one of five K.K.'s, customized by Lujie Lesovsky and Emil Deidt in 1948.

The yellow #19 Offy was driven by Ted Duncan and Johnnie Parsons.

Ted Duncan was involved in an accident at Rockford, Illinois on June 17, 1948 when the Pawl car left the track, striking two spectators, Ralph Brown (38) and his son Robert (17) killing both of them. After the accident Duncan had problems driving the #19 car.

Pawl sold the car to Angelo Howerton. Howerton only ran the car a few times before selling it to Oklahoma oil magnate and Champ car owner H.A. (Harry Allen) Chapman for his driver, Jack Penwell.

Chapman sold the car in the early 50s to Mike McGreevy who painted it purple and white #86, powered by an Offy.

B.C.R.A. owner Charlie Nelson was the next owner before selling the chassis to Dave Heltman. Heltman ran it as a blue #44 V8-60.

Ed Copple ran the seasoned K.K. as a white, purple and orange Falcon in B.C.R.A.

The car was last owned by Dick Gifford of Reno, Nevada in 1981.

Top Photo: Jack Penwell in the former Pawl car in 1950.

Lower Left: Jerry Bellville in Ed Copple's car in 1970. Some of the Deidt and Lesovsky bodywork is still in evidence.   J.M. Collection

Lower Right: Johnnie Parsons skies the clay at Walsh Stadium in Johnny Pawl's Offy 1949.

Mike McGreevy in the former Johnny Pawl chassis in 1956 at Bay Meadows.

◀

Jack Whelan Offy

This car became famous nationally in 1957 when piloted by midget racing great, Clark "Shorty" Templeman.

Templeman campaigned the car across the country from Freeport, Long Island to Saugus, California.

He ran the car on everything from tight 1/5 mile asphalt tracks to the one-mile dirt tracks like DuQuoin, Illinois.

The car carried a number of rather unusual paint jobs. Once it was painted gray and red, on another occasion it was painted pale blue, yellow and white.

Northern California sprint and midget driver, Cliff Blackwell, bought the car from Jack Whelan in 1962 or 1963. The car was painted black, white and red with a #1 on a checkered flag background.

Cliff ran the car for about two years. He sold the Offy engine to Moe Goff and took the car back to Chicago and sold it to Danny Kladis.

Danny Kladis cut the car in half and stretched it to accommodate a Falcon engine!

Cliff said Kladis told him his son was going to drive the car. The current location of the car is unknown.

Middle Photo: Clark "Shorty" Templeman in Jack Whelan's Offy at Trenton in 1957.

Bottom Photo: Cliff Blackwell in the former Whelan Offy in 1962.
J.M. Collection

Dee Toran 7-11

This car was like no other Kurtis - Kraft. The entire car was covered with 24 carat gold leaf! Instead of a number it had a pair of dice that could be read as seven and eleven.

This car was owned by a shadowy character who seemed to appear and disappear at different tracks all over the country.

Stories about Dee Toran's floating crap games and brushes with the law are legendary in the racing fraternity.

Toran sold the little Offy to an Eastern car owner named (?) Wolfgang who ran it in the same trim.

Wolfgang sold it to Charlie Sacks who painted it pink and black with gold trim powered by an Offy.

The midget has been restored to the Charlie Sacks colors.

▶

Dee Toran in his goldleafed 7-11 Offy.

Pre - war great, Ernie Gesell in the Wolfgang Offy at Williams Grove.

Eddie Sachs in the Charlie Sacks' car.

Joe Bertoncini V8-60

This blue and white V8-60, owned by Central Valley car owner Joe Bertoncini was campaigned in U.R.A. by drivers like Jimmy Bryan and Billy Cantrell. Bertoncini sold the car to Lou LaSpina in B.C.R.A.

LaSpina raced the Kurtis as a blue and white #84 V8-60.

Louie said he sold the car in Arizona, but he could not remember the buyer's name.

Billy Cantrell forgot more about racing than most drivers learned in a lifetime! Billy in the Bertoncini V8-60.   J.C. Collection

Hank Schloeder's Golden Arrow

Any race fan from the East Coast can attest to the electrifying, come from the back performances of Ed "Dutch" Schaefer in Hank "Slim" Schloeder's famous "Golden Arrow".

Tony Bonadies drove the car for a time but it was Ed "Dutch" Schaefer who will always be identified with the gold #6 Offy as its steady driver.

The car was sold to Ralph Smiley who also campaigned it in A.R.D.C.

The car has been restored by the current owner, John Gibbons (1983).

Top: Ed "Dutch" Schaefer in Hank "Slim" Schloeder's "Golden Arrow".

Bottom: Bill Hughes in Ralph Smiley's "Golden Arrow".

Walt and Charlie Booth V8-60

In 1956 Walt Booth was listed as the owner of this car. At the time it was a blue car with flames and was powered by a V8-60 engine.

From 1958 to 1964 Walt Booth was registered as the owner and the car experienced a number of engine changes that included a V8-60, Mercury Outboard and Chevy II.

Over the years the exterior of the car was painted red, purple to pink and black with polka dots!

Walt and Charlie were listed as the registered owners from 1966-67. Charlie was listed as the sole owner from 1968-69.

Don Sparks bought the car in 1970 and painted the Chevy II black and orange #77. Sparks only owned the car a year before selling it to Billy DeChamps who ran it as a blue and white #28 powered by a Chevy II.

DeChamps sold it to Sam Hucke who painted it red and white #24. Hucke ran the car until 1974, at that point the car dropped out of sight.

Top Photo: Charlie Booth in the Walt Booth V8-60, Oakland Indoors 1963. **J.M. Collection**

Bottom Photo: Chuck Gurney in Sam Hucke's Chevy II in 1974, the last year it ran. **J.M. Collection**

Duane Carter's "Speed Age" Special

Duane Carter's beautiful blue and silver Offy was an after market creation of Curly Wetteroth and Emil Deidt.

When midget racing slowed to a crawl in the early 1950s Duane sold the car to Tony Caccia.

Caccia kept the car a short time before ill health forced the sale of the car to Montgomeryville, Pennsylvania quarryman, Harry Hespell.

Hespell ran the car as a light blue Offy with a goldleafed #1.

Len Duncan drove the car for years and became strongly identified with the blue car.

Bobby Marshman, part of the Hespell race team, got a turn at the wheel and drove "Jolly" Cholly Hoff's red #65 Offy, the next owner.

Hoff loved racing but his dental practice limited his ability to travel with the car.

Boyce Holt of Marion, Indiana purchased the Offy and ran it as a blue #20. Sonny Ates was his driver.

Holt transferred ownership to John Hajduk who painted it pearl #20. The car's finest hour came at the Houston Astrodome in 1969 when Tom Bigelow won the Grand Prix and pocketed the lions share of the $63,000.00 purse!

In 1971 Danny Frye got the car and ran it with a Chevy II in S.L.A.R.A. Danny sold the aging K.K. to Doug Craig of Levittown, Pennsylvania who updated the car, completely changing the Deidt/Wetteroth look.

The next owner was Steve Howard. When Steve lost his life in a sprint car accident the car was sold to Mike McLaughlin in 1975.

The Moore Brothers of Moline, Illinois currently own the chassis and body parts in an unrestored condition (1996).

Above: Duane Carter in the immaculate, "Speed Age" Special at Pomona in 1950.

Top Left: Multiple A.R.D.C. Champion, Len Duncan in the Harry Hespell Offy at Hatfield, Pennsylvania in 1955.

Center Left: Sonny Ates in Boyce Holt's car at Daytona in 1964.

Lower Far Left: Whitewater, Wisconsin's Tom Bigelow in the Hajduk Offy at Hales Corners in 1968.

Lower Left: The ill fated Steve Howard and the former Duane Carter "Speed Age" Special 1974.

Cheesman Offy

This was a deep blue and white Offy owned by Bill Cheesman, driven in A.R.D.C. by Lloyd Christopher and Ted Tappett.

The car was sold to Hank Green who ran it as a white and red #98 Offy, reminiscent of J.C. Agajanian's paint job.

Midget veterans Johnny Thomson and Johnnie Parsons graced the cockpit of this car.

Green sold the Kurtis to Denver's Bus Osborne who, in time transferred ownership to another Denverite named Oberholster.

A 1959 photo by Leroy Byers shows Vern Meeks in the car at Grand Junction, Colorado when it was a white #88 Offy sponsored by "Foreign Cars Inc."

Oberholster moved to California and sold the car on the West Coast.

Top: Johnnie Tolan at Terre Haute in the Hank Green car, still in the Cheesman trim.

Center: Vern Meeks in the Oberholster Offy at Grand Junction, Colorado in 1959.

Below: Lloyd Christopher in the Cheesman Offy in 1949.

Walt Johnson Offy

Walt Johnson, a long time U.S.A.C. official, owned this well maintained gray and red #36 Offy driven by Joe Garson.

Walt sold the car to Gene Cox who also ran it as a gray and red #36 with both a V8-60 and Offy engine.

Dudley Stauffacher purchased the car in 1958. He put a V8-60 in the chassis and campaigned it until 1963.

Another Southern Californian, Jim Devitt bought the car and ran it as a #89 V8-60.

Chuck Crawford from the Fresno area bought the K.K. in 1965, removed the V8-60 and put a Falcon in the maroon #89X. Crawford's driver, Dick Carmichael, lost his life in the car at Chico, California on July 2, 1966. Carmichael flipped out over the first turn embankment and crashed into a parked grader.

The car was sold in Northern California to Frank Lipari in 1967. Lipari originally painted the Falcon powered car, red #66 and campaigned it in B.C.R.A. In later years he ran the car as a blue #9.

Lipari's driver, Jack Walker said Lipari's brother inherited the car after Frank's death.

Walter believed it was rusting away on his farm in Kansas.

Bottom Left: Joe Garson in Walt Johnson's Offy at Saugus.

Bottom Right: Bob Cortner in Gene Cox's Offy in 1957.

Top: Dick Carmichael in Chuck Crawford's Falcon powered car in 1966.
J.M. Collection

Center: Jack Walker in the Frank Lipari Falcon in 1968.
J.M. Collection

Smart/ Bonadies Offy

This car was owned by, driver, Tony Bonadies and Tommy Smart.

The car was painted a rather drab gray and blue, #4 powered by an Offy.

Len Duncan, Bert Brooks and naturally, Tony Bonadies, campaigned the car.

In 1954 the car was sold to Bill Zerillo who ran it with the same colors, number and engine. Tony Romit was his steady driver.

In 1965 another resident of the Bronx, Tony Madonia, got the car and ran it as the "Ali-Jon" Offy.

Tony Madonia, (aka), "Sonny Saunders", wrecked the car badly at Danbury and it was sold to Tommy Goggin.

In a recent conversation with Marty Himes he told me this car has been restored as another famous car. If this is the case it is unfortunate.

Top: Al Herman in the Bill Zerillo Offy.

Center: Tony Madonia in the "Ali-Jon" Offy 1965.

Below: Len Duncan in the Tommy Smart Offy.

Lenny Gonsel's 1947 Kurtis

Lenny Gonsel bought this car in 1947. Lenny was especially fond of a yellow and red paint scheme and his cars, dubbed "Yellow Birds", were usually painted this way.

Gonsel had many accomplished drivers in his car, including 1955 Indy winner, Bob Sweikert.

In 1950 Woody Brown won the B.C.R.A. Indoor and Overall Championship in Lenny's car.

Sim Clark purchased the car and ran it as a red #96 powered by a V8-60. Sim later switched to a Chevy II powerplant.

Some of the finest drivers in B.C.R.A. drove for Sim. Men like Dick Atkins, Hank Butcher and Tommy Copp.

The car was sold to Rich Lawson who campaigned it as an orange and white #43 Chevy II.

The cars last owner was Tom Whittington. The car was a red #36 Chevy II.

Whittington was involved in a crash at Madera Speedway in 1976 that destroyed the car.

Top: Woody Brown won the B.C.R.A. Indoor and Overall Championship for Lenny Gonsel in 1950. J.C. Collection

BottomLeft: 1964 and 1965 B.C.R.A. Overall Champion, Dick Atkins in Sim Clark's Chevy II in 1965. J.M. Collection

Bottom Right: Tom Whittington in the former Gonsel K.K. in 1976, the year it was destroyed at Madera, California.

Walton and French Drake

The famous Merrill Walton and George French maroon and white #56 Drake, driven by Billy Cantrell, in 1947, was sold to Joe Ellis who ran it in U.R.A. until 1950.

Years later it turned up in the hands of Pete Bitroff who ran it as a #6 Offy in U.S.R.C.

The current owner of the car is unknown.

Billy Cantrell prepares to qualify the Walton and French Drake. U.R.A. President, Roscoe Turner stands next to the car.

Angelo Howerton #33 V8-60

Angelo Howerton had a team of two V8-60 K.K.'s.

The #33 car, originally bought from Clay Smith and Danny Jones in California, was sold to Max Willis of Wood River, Illinois.

The car was in turn sold to Arnie Knepper who sold it to Danny Frye.

Danny told me he sold it to Melvin Rice in Millstat, Illinois, the same fellow who bought the famous #55 Mensing Offy.

Rice committed suicide by hanging himself in his garage, between his two prized midget race cars!

An unidentified driver in the Max Willis #7 passes Burt Wilson.

Julius Holman V8-60

This Kurtis was a 1947 U.R.A. car operated by Julius Holman as a black #58 V8-60.

The car was purchased by Phil Casanta who transferred ownership to Freddie Chaparro in 1955.

Freddie ran it in U.R.A. with a V8-60 powerplant.

Karl Kocen acquired the car from Chaparro and later sold it to Paul Zeumer.

The midget moved to Northern California under the ownership of B.C.R.A. driver, Larry Moore. Moore campaigned the Kurtis as a red #56 V8-60.

Perennial B.C.R.A. car owner, Tom Dupont, owned the car for a time before transferring ownership to Bill Evitt who ran it as a gold and black #43 Chevy II.

The current disposition of the car is unknown.

Below: Freddie Chaparro in his own V8-60 in 1956.

Smith and Jones

This famous red and white V8-60 owned by cam grinder, Clay Smith and Danny Jones was driven by Allen Heath and Walt Faulkner in the tough U.R.A. Red Circuit.

Smith and Jones sold the car to Doug Caruthers who ran it as a purple #33 V8-60 with the great Jimmy Bryan as his steady driver.

Don Cameron bought the car from Doug Caruthers and ran it as a blue and white V8-60.

Jim Chini believes he sold it to George Talents who ran the car as a V-4 Chevy.

Pete Bitroff owned the car in the late 60's. The car was a white V-4 Chevy.

Jim Watson of Simi Valley was the last known owner of the car. Watson ran the car as a white and red #68 V-4 Chevy in 1972.

Top Right: One of the greatest drivers in the history of racing, Jimmy Bryan, in Doug Caruthers' purple #33 V8-60.   J.C. Collection

Center Right: Jim Watson was the last owner of the car.
                                                                      J.M. Collection

Lower Right: Allen Heath beats a hasty retreat from the wounded Smith and Jones V8-60 at Balboa in 1949.

Below: Don Cameron in Doug Caruthers' car shortly before he bought it.

Moreland Visel Offy

The Visel Offy was an attractive metallic blue #24, driven by Johnnie Parsons.

The car was bought by Leonard Faas in June of 1947. It was his light blue, white and red #16 car driven by Walt Faulkner.

In September of 1947 Faas sold the car to Bruce and Everett Johnston.

The blue and white #66 Offy was campaigned by Mack Hellings.

Bruce Johnston stretched the midget into a sprint car and sold it to Johnnie Pouelsen.

The current owner is not known.

Above: Mack Hellings in Bruce Johnston's Offy at Langhorne in 1947.

Left: Johnnie Parsons in Moreland Visel's Offy at Culver City in 1947. J.C. Collection

Below: Walt Faulkner in Leonard Faas' car. J.C. Collection

Joe Brugnolotti #55 Offy

In 1949 this car was driven by Buddy Chase. Chase scored his first victory in the car at Islip in 1949. In September of 1950 he took a wild ride at Morristown and came away from the incident with nothing more than a broken finger.

Brugnolotti sold the car to Al Leutone. The car ran as a #20. Al Keller was one of his drivers.

Brugnolotti got the car back and replaced his #55.

In 1953 the car was sold to Tommy Cochrane who called it the Ridge Offy, named after the Bay Ridge section of Brooklyn that he called home.

Ed and Bill Mataka from Maplewood, New Jersey bought the car from Cochrane. It was painted yellow #11 with an Offy.

In late August of 1962 Mario Andretti became their steady driver. One year later in August 1963 Andretti made A.R.D.C. history by winning three main events in one day! Two of those mains coming at Hatfield and one at Flemington.

The Mataka's sold the car to Larry McCoy who ran it as a #21 in A.R.D.C. in 1967.

According to Harry Stryker it is owned by a gentleman named Irwin Schumacher who resides in Idaho (1998).

Top: Indy winner, Mario Andretti in the Mataka Brothers' Offy.

Bottom: Al Keller in Al Leutone's Offy.

Below: Buddy Chase in the Joe Brugnolotti Offy.

Roy Leslie Continental Airlines Offy

This beautiful and famous blue and white #62 Offy was driven to the 1947 R.M.M.R.A. championship by Johnny Tolan.

The car was sold to Joe Giba who also raced it as a #62 Offy. Later he replaced the Offy with an outboard engine.

When Joe Giba could no longer drive, he sold the car to Jack Skellinger.

Skellinger relocated to southern California and sold the car to Ray Jimenez who installed a Pinto engine.

Max Sweeney lost his life in this car at Ascot Speedway in 1982.

The car is presently owned by Lou Loucart in Burbank (1999).

Above: Joe Giba in the former Roy Leslie Offy.

Below: Johnnie Tolan and Roy Leslie accept their 1947 R.M.M.R.A. Championship trophy.

Bill Kenz and Roy Leslie V8-60.

This hot little black #67 V8-60 was driven to the 1950 R.M.M.R.A. championship by Sonny Coleman.

Leslie sold the car to Midwestern car owner, Frank Pavese.

Willie Wildhaber and Bob Tattersall drove the car.

Pavese sold the car to Matt Schneider who was the last owner to run the car in competition.

Bill Kenz told Leroy Byers that a gentleman in Detroit was restoring the car (1997).

Top: Bob Hauck in the Matt Schneider Chevy II.

Center: Danny Kaldis in the #67 former Kenz - Leslie V8-60. Willie Wildhaber is in the #27 and car owner, Frank Pavese, is the gentleman in the hat.

Below: Sonny Coleman and Bill Kenz pick up the hardware for winning the 1950 R.M.M.R.A. Championship.

Ray Crawford Offy

This car ran for years on the West Coast with ex-firefighter pilot and supermarket owner, Ray Crawford at the wheel.

Crawford usually had the Offy painted red #49.

When Ray retired he sold the car to Russ Moynagh who painted it black #79 with Offy Power.

The last known owner, in 1962, was Bernie Schecter.

Ray Crawford in his own car at Culver City in 1948.
J.C. Collection

John Zink Kit Car

In 1947 John Zink put together a K.K. kit car, assembled by Felix Graves, Buzz Barton and John Zink at a cost of $8,000.00.

In the early part of 1948 Buzz Barton barnstormed the #2 Offy on the West Coast.

Years later, John Zink instructed mechanic, Denny Moore, to turn the midget into a dragster!

Th effort was a failure.

What was left of the car was sold to Ed Silk who saved the car and sold it in 1961.

The current location of the car is unknown.

One of the most underrated drivers in the history of the sport was cigar chomping, Buzz Barton from Chickasha, Oklahoma. Buzz is in John Zink's Offy.

185

Joe Subjak #54 Offy

This car was originally owned by Bob Wilke's mechanic, Joe Subjak.

Subjak sold the car to Eastern driving ace, Joe Sostillio. Sostillio ran it as a #54.

Sostillio sold the car to another New Englander, speed shop proprietor, Ed Stone.

The car ran as a white and red #2 Offy. Johnny Kay occasionally drove the car.

Stone transferred ownership to Wally White who continued the Subjak - Sostillio tradition and ran it as a #54.

The next owner, Stan Bartkiewicz ran it as a #54 Offy . Across its hood was written "Cecilia G.". His driver, Ray Brown won several important races in the car at Williams Grove in 1962.

Hud Meyer contended that Fred Bartkiewicz was involved in a horrific accident around this time and the car was destroyed.

Others say the car was sold to a man named Neally and was restored by Charles Schell.

Top: The Ed Stone race team with John Bernardi in the #55 car and Dick Shubruk in the #2 car, formerly the Sostillio Offy.

Center: Joe Sostillio in his own car.

Below: Fred Bartkiewicz in the "Cecilia G." Offy at Danbury, Connecticut in 1962.

Ray Nichels' Offy

This famous car ran with a polished aluminum body wearing the #2.

Indy vet, Paul Russo was a steady driver for Ray.

In 1948 Nichels sold the car to Tulsa, Oklahoma businessman, John Zink who numbered it #3.

The car had an illustrious career with drivers like Cecil Green, Jimmy Reece and Jud Larson behind the wheel.

The car ran as a #2, #44, #8, #25, and a #52. It is still owned by John Zink (1997).

Above: Car owner, Ray Nichels poses with his driver, Indy vet, Paul Russo.

Below: Little Cecil Green at Milwaukee in the John Zink Offy in 1949. Zink called this car, "John's other box".

Sam Hanks' Offies

Sam Hanks had two black Offies, #2 and #5 that he campaigned in 1948.

In 1949 Sam sold both cars to Bob Clement of Detroit.

Clement sold the former Hanks #2 car to Bill Rao who painted it as red #25 with Offy power.

Wally Hostetler was his steady driver.

Bill Rao later sold the car to Harry Hawkins, who numbered the car thirty-five. Hostetler also drove for him.

The #5 car was sold to Ray Bohlander who ran the car as a red #4 Offy. The Offy engine tag was #230.

The Bohlander car was a fixture in the Midwest with Gene Hartley handling the driving chores.

It is rumored the Bohlander car may be in the basement of the Indianapolis Speedway Museum.

Sam Hanks in his own #5 car at DuQuoin, Illinois on the mile in 1948.   J.C. Collection

Top Photo: Sam Hanks in his #2 car at West 16th Street in 1948.

Center Photo: Gene Hartley at DuQuoin in 1958 driving the Ray Bohlander #4 Offy. The former Sam Hanks #5 car.

Bottom Photo: Wally Hostetler in the Rao Offy at Williams Grove in 1954.

Clancy & Dasher Offy

The Clancy & Dasher Offy was sold to Ted Wise then to Ed Hood, who ran the car as a #5 Offy.

The car became the famous Dallas Garman #5 driven by Gene Weyant, Billy Douglas, Steve Orme and Jerry Kemp.

Billy Douglas in the Dallas Garman Offy in 1968.

Cecil Zent in the Elza Bynum #99 at Walsh Stadium.

Elza Bynum's #66 & #99 Offies

Elza Bynum bought his #66 and #99 midgets in 1948.

The cars were driven by Speedy Matheny and Cecil Green.

In 1949 Bynum sold the cars to Speedy Matheny and mechanic, Tommy Flanders.

The #99 car was numbered nine and the #66 car was numbered eight.

Matheny sold the cars to the promoter of Dallas Fair Park, Henry Watson.

The current disposition of the cars is unknown.

Howard Kelley #13 V8-60

It is obvious Howard Kelley was not a superstitious man. The car he ran in U.R.A. in the 1950s was a green #13 V8-60!

The car went through the hands of Don Lodes 1953-1955, Bob Hill 1956-1958, Bill Taul 1958-1960 and Norm Rapp 1961-1962 before Chuck Freedlun acquired the car in 1962.

After three sessions Freedlun sold the car to Bud Jackson in 1965.

Jackson replaced the V8-60 with a Chevy II and did a little body styling by removing the headrest on the black and gold #25 car.

In 1971 Bud sold the car to Terry McCreary, a resident of Reno, Nevada.

Terry Petersen, a fellow resident of the Silver State purchased the car in 1973.

He was the last person to run the car competitively.

Top Photo: Chuck Freedlun in his #55 V8-60 in 1962.

Center Photo: Terry McCreary in the car in 1972.   J.M. Collection

Bottom Photo: Lloyd Nygren in Bud Jackson's Chevy II in 1966.

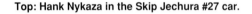

Hank Green #76 K.K.

Leroy Warriner said this car was the #27 car owned by Skip Jechura in which Hank Nykaza lost his life at Milwaukee.

Jechura sold the car to Bill Lloyd and he put Paul Howe in the car.

Howe lost his life in the car at South Bend, Indiana!

Lloyd sold the car to Hank Green and it became his black and gold #76 car that Leroy drove.

Leroy said he sold the car in Australia to Don Mackay.

Youthful Australian sensation, Jeff Freeman lost his life in the car in 1965.

Don Mackay sold the car to Eric Kydd.

Top: Hank Nykaza in the Skip Jechura #27 car.

Center: Leroy Warriner in the Hank Green #76 Offy.

Below: Jeff Freeman in the Don Mackay car in Australia.

Harry Shilling V8-60

In 1947 Harry Shilling owned this beautifully maintained white and red V8-60.

It was driven by Johnny Soares, currently the promoter of Petaluma Speedway in Northern California.

Shilling sold the car to Buzz Balfour in 1950. Balfour ran the car as a #9 V8-60.

Charlie Lawlor bought the car in 1953 and campaigned it for seven seasons.

Fred Papina bought the car from Lawlor in 1961. His car was usually painted blue and yellow.

After three seasons Fred Papina sold the car to Henry Rossi in 1964.

Rossi, like Lawlor, campaigned the aging K.K. for seven seasons.

The car was yellow for several years then Henry painted it gold.

In 1968 the V8-60 was updated with Chevy II power. Rossi last ran the car in 1970.

The car sat several years until Jack Wilson purchased it in 1973.

The car was sold in 1975 and the registered owner was Virginia Palmer.

Tom Palmer told me the car was badly damaged at San Jose in 1977 and the chassis is rusting away behind his house.

He added that there is some question in his mind that this is, indeed, a Kurtis chassis (1998).

Below: Johnny Soares in the Harry Shilling V8-60 at Fresno in 1947. Photo courtesy "BCRA the First 50 Years" by Tom Motter.

Quince Gibson #9 Offy

This car was the blue #9 in Gibson's two car team. Bud Camden was the driver.

The car went through the hands of Leo Hallick and Carl Guth, from Kansas City, before it became part of the Jack Cunningham stable.

The black #14 Cunningham Offy, driven by the ageless Joe Walters, became a familiar sight in the Midwest.

Cunningham owned the car for nearly nine years before selling it to Bill Darnell who also ran the car as a #14 Offy.

According to Danny Frye, when Darnell died his son inherited the car (1998).

Top: The graying, Joe Walters in the Darnell Offy that was originally the #9 Gibson Offy.

Bottom: The two car Quince Gibson team at Olympic Stadium. Mac McHenry is in the #5 and Buzz Barton is in the #9 car.

Frank "Satan" Brewer's V8-60

This pretty little blue and white #99 V8-60 was a familiar sight at U.R.A. races in Southern California with owner- driver, Frank "Satan" Brewer at the wheel.

Brewer was an Australian who came to California to race and stayed.

In the early 1950s Brewer moved back to Australia, with his car.

Frank sold the car to Hedley McGee of Sydney who put a new chassis 6" longer than the Brewer chassis, under the car to accommodate a 6 cyl. Holden engine. The once pretty little Kurtis looked grotesque.

The car was sold to promoter, Kym Bonython who transferred ownership to Harry Neale.

Neale was killed in the car at Claremont, Australia and the car was sold to Ted Dark.

Dark put Howard Revell, son of Ray Revell, in the car.

The car is being restored by a relative of Ted Dark, but according to my source in Australia, the original chassis was removed and destroyed.

Top photo: Frank "Satan" Brewer in his V8-60.

Center Photo: Frank "Satan" Brewer and his blue and white #99.

Bottom Photo: Howard Revell in Ted Dark's homely stretched Kurtis in 1969.

Marv Edwards' second K.K.

Marv Edwards' second car was a short wheelbase car driven by Howard Kelley.

In the early 1960s the car, usually a plain run of the mill looking machine, underwent a metamorphosis and became the beautiful white, red, blue and silverleafed #98 "Willard Battery Special" driven by Parnelli Jones.

Those privileged to witness the races at Ascot in the early 1960s between A.J. Foyt, in Jack London's Offy, and Parnelli Jones in the Edwards car, can attest to the fact that this little car was one of the best handling K.K. midgets ever built.

A.J. Foyt bought the car from Edwards and painted it orange with the #83.

Foyt only ran the car on a few occasions, notably, at the Houston Astrodome midget races in 1969, '70 and '72, which he won in 1970.

Foyt sold the car at auction for nearly $85,000 several years later.

Above: Howard Kelley in the Marv Edwards "short car" in 1954.

Below: Parnelli Jones in the Marv Edwards Offy at Ascot.
J.C. Collection

Vern Boone V8-60

Vern Boone, the grandfather of U.S.A.C. driver Bobby Boone, owned a #90 blue and white V8-60 that he ran in U.R.A.

Rod Simms and Hal Minyard were two of his drivers.

In the early 1950s Boone sold the car for $2,500.00 to a promoter who was planning to run a series of races in England.

Vern said he didn't think the man who purchased the car was Dan Topping.

The name of the promoter, and the current whereabouts of the car is unknown.

Rod Simms in the Vern Boone V8-60 at Culver City in 1947.

J.C. Collection

Jack Fresholtz Offy

The Jack Fresholtz Offy was driven by the likes of Mack Hellings, Gordon Reid, Cal Niday, Bob Pankratz and Frank Armi.

The Fresholtz car was usually painted maroon and gold or gold and purple.

The car was sold to Bob Bogan who kept the Offy engine and sold the car to Bill Henning who ran it as a cream #53 V8-60. Freddie Chaparro was his driver.

It is unclear what became of the car after Henning sold it to Lefty Dressen.

Frank Armi in the Jack Fresholtz Offy in 1956.

Baker & Frincke V8-60

The Baker and Frincke V8-60 was a 1948 Kurtis - Kraft driven by Byron Counts and the great Jimmy Bryan.

It debuted as a red #94 car in the U.R.A. Red Circuit. The following year it carried the #21 and was painted metallic copper and metallic blue.

The car was sold to Art Bagnall and Bill Payson in 1953.

Bob and Don Weaver acquired the car in 1954 and it ran as a yellow and blue V8-60.

It appears the Weaver Brothers ran the car until at least 1956.

Jimmy Bryan in the Baker & Frincke V8-60.

196

"Red" Marley #88 Offy

The "Red" Marley Offy had to be one of the prettiest midgets to race the Midwest.

The car was painted cherry red with a goldleafed #88 in block numerals. The sponsors name, "Drewry Special" was goldleafed on the hood.

Gene Hartley, Forrest Parker and Red Hamilton were three of the outstanding drivers that drove this famous car.

The car was sold to Chuck Benda who also ran it as a #88 and #89.

The car was painted yellow and the sponsor was "Chuck's Excavating". Arizona driver, Don Davis was one of his drivers.

In a recent telephone conversation it was learned that Paul Baines of Mattoon, Illinois may have purchased the car from Chuck Benda.

Above: Don Davis in Chuck Benda's car.

Below: Gene Hartley in "Red" Marley's #88 Offy.

George Newnam Offy

This transitional car fits, uncomfortably, into the Kurtis - Kraft history.

In 1952 George Newnam, the owner of Norden Steering ordered a chassis.

Shortly after work was begun on the chassis Johnny Pawl bought the company!

The chassis left the Kurtis - Kraft plant in L.A., partially completed.

Pawl finished the car in Crown Point, Indiana and shipped it back to Newnam.

Pawl never numbered his chassis so Newnam received the car from Pawl, without a chassis I.D. number.

George ran the white and blue Offy with Lowell Sachs as his steady driver.

George owned the car until his death.

It is believed his son still owns the car (1998).

George Newnam's car at an Ascot vintage event in the 1980s.

The M-100 Midget Roadsters

BUILT BY
KURTIS - KRAFT
— INC. —
LOS ANGELES
CALIF.   19--

— Chapter Ten —
The M-100 Midget Roadsters

In the fall of 1956 Frank Kurtis began his last production of midget race cars.

These cars - designated as the M-100 series were scaled down versions of the famous 500-G Indy roadster.

The M-100 employed a space frame chassis with cross torsion suspension and telescopic shocks. The engine was offset 5 1/2" to the left, which transferred the weight to the left by 15%. The cars overall length was 123" by 28" wide and a sleek 26" in height.

The first roadster midget delivered to Ashley Wright, in mid-December 1956, was hastily prepared for its maiden race on December 30th at Saugus, California by crew chief Larry Crim.

Originally, the Offy powered car was painted white with a black #57. Later that year the car received Wrights' familiar goldleafed starburst containing the #57.

Pavement specialist Bob Gregg of Portland, Oregon set the quick time and finished second in the dash in the car.

Hopes were high for the sleek pavement predator. In his heat race several cars spun in front of Gregg. In an attempt to miss one car, Gregg put the roadster into the fence and out of the race.

The M-100 weighed 900 pounds, ready to race. This was about 30 pounds heavier than a conventional midget - a fact that didn't go unnoticed by weight conscious car owners.

A more grievous fault of the car was its poor handling characteristics on rough dirt surfaces.

Bob Gregg explained that the front axle bottomed out on the chassis due to insufficient allowance for travel.

When the axle bottomed out it caused an immediate loss of steering as the front end washed out.

Initially, buyers like Tassi Vatis in the East, Ed Walker in Denver and Ray Tomaseski in the Midwest restricted their racing to the macadam tracks and did just fine with Frank's new low slung thunderbug.

There was a renaissance in midget racing in the mid to late 1950s but car owners couldn't see any reason to own two cars when the original K.K. race car was perfect for both dirt and asphalt!

Frank Kurtis became a victim of his own genius.

Only ten of the roadsters were put into production and only six were completed by Kurtis. Three of the remaining cars were sold to Charley Peck and one was sold to Kurtis employee, Ron Ward.

Through a strange twist, the car that was designated as the second chassis was the first chassis to be completed.

Ashley Wright was in California and the plant hurried his car through the line so he could showcase the new creation at Saugus.

Serial Numbers

An explanation of the chassis numbering system, employed on the roadsters is warranted.

The first number of the three digit serial number designates the chassis number.

The second and third numbers reflect the year of manufacture.

DATE	OWNER	SERIAL#
1957	Ray Tomaseski	157
1957	Ashley Wright	257
1957	Tassi Vatis	357
1957	Ed Walker	457
1958	Ernie Alvarado	558
1959	Hank Green	659

Ray Tomaseski Roadster

The orange #1 Ray Tomaseski roadster helped Shorty Templeman win his second straight U.S.A.C. National Championship in 1957.

Ray sold the car to George Williford from Ohio with George's son Dick doing the driving. After he finished campaigning the car he sold it to Al "Wimpy" Vorber.

Vorber had it for some years before selling it to Eastern car and engine broker - Jim Etters.

Etters sold the sleek creation to Junior Dryer (1997).

Dick Williford in the former Tomaseski roadster.
Note the "T" in the front pusher.

Three time U.S.A.C. National Champion, "Shorty" Templeman poses with Ray Tomaseski and his wife at Soldier Field in Chicago in 1957.

Ashley Wright Roadster

This car must be the most famous of the Kurtis roadster midgets.

The car first made its appearance at Saugus in December of 1956.

The car was driven by, Bob Gregg, Len Sutton, Tony Bettenhausen and Shorty Templeman.

In 1958 it was sold to flamboyant, Eastern businessman, Bruce Homeyer. Homeyer repainted the car red #27 "Konstant Hot Special" with the same gold splash motif used by Wright.

Tony Romit was Homeyer's steady driver, although Eddie Sachs took a turn behind the wheel at the Trenton 100.

Homeyer sold the car to Tony Bonadies who also ran it as a #27.

The car became part of Tony's estate when he lost his life in another midget at Williams Grove on July 5, 1965.

It is believed this car is in the possession of his son who resides in Florida and operates a Speed Shop.

Tough, Tony Bonadies in the Bruce Homeyer roadster. Bonadies later bought the car.

Bob Gregg in the brand new Ashley Wright roadster in December of 1956.

Tassi Vatis Roadster

This red and black #9 was driven with flawless perfection by pavement specialist, Tony Bonadies.

When Vatis decided to sell the car he transferred ownership to A.R.D.C. veteran, "Pop" Sincerbaux.

Sincerbaux painted it red and black #49. It was called the "Airway Cab Special."

The driver was his son, Chuckie Stane (his racing name).

The present owner of the car is Freddie Charles (Heydenreich), the father of Johnny Heydenreich (1982).

Top: Tony Bonadies in the Tassi Vatis red and black roadster midget.

Center: The second owner of the car was "Pop" Sincerbaux. Johnny Kay is the driver.

Bottom: Freddie Charles (Heydenreich) in the former Tassi Vatis car.
Arnie de Brier Photo

Ed Walker Roadster

After Ed Walker finished campaigning his blue #89 roadster all over the country he sold his car to fellow Denverite, Jack Skellinger.

Skellinger relocated in California and was trying to sell this car in the early 1970's for $1,500.00, but couldn't find a buyer!

Ken Hillberg thought Cal Niday restored the car and sold it to someone on the East Coast?

Andy Furci in the Ed Walker roadster at West 16th Street in 1957.

Ernie Alvarado Roadster

This Southern California car was owned by Ernie Alvarado. The proprietor of a camera store, he painted his car, "Kodak Yellow."

Bill Homeier and Joe Garson drove the car for Alvarado.

The car was sold to Michael "Mick" Nagy in Racine, Wisconsin. It was a yellow #29 Offy.

After Nagy's death in 1963, the car was sold to Tony Saylor of Joliet, Illinois.

Saylor sold the car to Mel Owens who transferred ownership to "Smokin" Joe Will.

Joe Will still owned the car in 1986.

Top: Gene Hartley at Milwaukee in Mick Nagy's car in 1960.

Center: Dick Atkins ran Tony Saylor's roadster on the mile at DuQuoin in 1966.

Bottom: Bill Homeier in the Ernie Alvarado roadster.

Charley Peck's Kit Cars

Charley Peck, the West Virginia fiberglass man noted for his "Shovel nose" after-market radiator shells found on so many K.K. upright midgets, purchased the last three M-100 roadsters.

The cars were partially assembled, less the labor intensive aluminum nose and tails.

Charley used his talent as a fiberglass specialist to re-create the nose and tail section of the cars in fiberglass.

Peck sold one of the cars to Arnie Knepper from Belleville, Illinois.

Knepper ran the car as a yellow and blue #30 Offy.

Paul Larson bought the car from Don Edmunds' collection of historic cars and restored it to the Knepper colors, but changed the number to #32.

Several years ago Paul Larson had the car for sale (1989).

It is unclear if Peck sold a car to Ed Silk in Denver, Colorado.

Ed Silk put together a pearl #91 Offy roadster for Glenn Scott, that Steve Troxell drove to the 1966 R.M.M.R.A. Championship. The car looks to be one of the Peck cars purchased from Kurtis - but I am not certain of this.

The car is now in the possession of racing photographer and car collector, Leroy Byers in Denver, Colorado.

The disposition of the last car purchased by Peck is unknown.

Steve Troxell in the Glenn Scott Offy roadster, in which he annexed the 1966 R.M.M.R.A. Championship. This car appears to be a Kurtis.

Paul Larson did a nice job of restoration of the ex-Knepper car, seen here at a vintage race at Ascot in the 1980's.

Arnie Knepper in his yellow and blue, Charley Peck M-100 in 1966 at Lakeside Speedway in Denver.

Hank Green Roadster

According to David Johnson, a correspondent in Australia, the beautiful black and silver leafed #76 roadster driven by Leroy Warriner is in the possession of Arthur Sollit in Brisbane, Australia (1989).

Leroy Warriner at Milwaukee in Hank Green's roadster in 1959.

Jerry Welton Roadster

The seventh of the ten Kurtis - Kraft M-100 roadsters was originally purchased by Kurtis employee, Ron Ward.

Jerry Welton bought the car and modified the front end by removing the cross torsion and replacing it with a transverse spring.

The modification gave the car a very stubby, unattractive appearance.

Welton also elected to use a supercharged Crosley engine instead of the preferred Offy.

The car resurfaced in the 1980s as a metallic blue and white #6 in the possession of John Moser from Washington State.

Jerry Welton in his Crosley powered M-100 Roadster at San Jose.

Chapter Eleven

The Sum of the Parts

Many people assume that all K.K. midgets looked alike. While it may be difficult, or impossible to identify many K.K. midgets, it is possible to identify many by various distinctive characteristics. In this section some of those key identifiers are discussed.

Flat Hood Line

The earliest K.K. midgets had a flat hood line that possessed little if any rake from the cowl to the radiator hoop.

Frank Kurtis told Gordon White he felt this was unattractive and he corrected it early in the production of the car.

Kurtis simply raised the cowl hoop to give it the look that we associate with the car.

No more than twenty of the first cars were fitted with the old style hood.

Cowl Flair

Shortly after the car was introduced, drivers and owners complained to Kurtis that the plastic windscreen, alone, lacked adequate protection from rocks and dirt, thrown from the rear tires of the cars.

The solution was called a cowl flair. A small, but intricately formed piece of aluminum that incorporated a compound bend.

The piece was fitted to the hood with screws and the windshield was attached.

Kurtis disliked making the flair, because he felt fabricating the piece was too labor intensive.

An after market sprung up among metal fabricators like Deidt, Lesovsky, Ewing, Fred Glass and Pankratz who built attractive hoods with a cowl flair built into them.

Above: Drivers preferred the modified hood with a built in cowl flair, like the one on the #10 Krech Offy. Manny Ayulo is the driver.

Left: The flat hood line is plainly evident in this photo of Lloyd Axel's car.

Louvers

Many K.K. midgets were louvered. The work might have been done in house by Rudy Capranica or it might have been subbed out to Art Ingalls' shop.

Louvers can be compared to fingerprints as a means of identification if the car has its original body panels.

When belly pans, hoods and engine side panels were replaced to accomodate modern engines, older original aluminum pans and side panels were sometimes included with the spare parts when the car was sold. These are the parts to check.

The restorer usually has some idea of who might have campaigned the car he owns.

If that is the case, a magnifier and a stack of old photos will soon answer your questions (See photos illustrating louver match on chassis #11).

Use common sense. If the car you have has the same number of louvers in the hood and on the right side engine panel as the target car, don't assume it is not the same if the belly pan doesn't match. One of the former owners may have replaced a front belly pan or rear belly pan.

Louvers should be used as one step in the investigative process in establishing authenticity, not as the sole means of identification.

I must also mention that the addition of an air scoop on the belly pan, though rare, is a great identifier.

The #3 Cheesman Offy driven by Ted Tappett and Lloyd Christopher had an air scoop on the left side of the car on the rear belly pan.

This scoop remained on the car through three different car owners, aiding in a positive identification of the car as it passed through the hands of Cheesman, Green and Oberholster. (See the Cheesman Offy p.172).

Carburetor "Bumps"

At the Kurtis plant Ernie Wheatley hammered out the left engine side panel to accommodate the Riley sidecraft carburetors.

Sometimes these convex, teardrop shaped structures, were singular and sometimes there were two units. Some were quite deep and some of these declivities were shallow.

This is an unreliable indicator for a restorer because this panel was usually discarded when a car was updated with fuel injection.

This is a good way to trace a car through its original, and subsequent owners, using photos of the car.

Dzus pads and Dzus Washers

The Dzus washer was attached to an aluminum panel when the hole, to accommodate the Dzus button, had worn through the aluminum making the hole oversized.

If you own a car that has some of the original side panels, nose, hood or tail, it is possible that a Dzus washer has been employed to repair a worn hole in the aluminum.

Compare photos of the target car and the car you own to see if any washers are in the same place. Dzus washers in the same location can be an indicator that your car and that earlier car might be the same.

On very early cars the hole for the Dzus pad is about 1/2" from the bottom of the cockpit side panel. The hole for the Dzus pad is about 1 1/2" down on the belly pan. Sometime after production of the thirtieth car the pad was welded to the frame so the hole on the cockpit panel and hole in the belly pan were an inch from the edge of the panel. This gave it more strength, and symmetry.

Notice the location of the 1/4 x 28 hex head bolts holding the side panels and belly pans in place on this very early car owned by Eddie Gdula. The earliest cars didn't employ the use of Dzus buttons.

Custom Bodies

Some K.K. midgets were re-bodied by after market fabricators. This makes identification rather simple!

The finest examples were produced by men like Lujie Lesovsky, Emil Deidt, Wayne Ewing, Bob Pankratz, Fred Glass and later Don Edmunds.

Charley Peck, from West Virginia, fabricated fiberglass shovel nosed radiator shells and "Booby" Logan in Detroit built similar radiator shells of aluminum.

Deidt and Lesovsky are responsible for building five cars in 1948; the Gerhardt #45 Offy, Johnny Pawl #19 Offy, Danny Quella #6 Offy, Balch #65 Offy and Sammy Bruno's #174 V8-60.

Wayne Ewing modified the Snook Offy and had a hand in building the Niday Offy. So talented was Ewing that a fellow worker proclaimed he could build an entire car body with a hammer and a dolly!

Bob Pankratz built the famous Pat Clancy, later the Davies' Offy. This car was so well camouflaged by Pankratz' innovative styling, that nobody realized the chassis was a K.K. until several years ago! Don Edmonds did some significant aluminum work on the beautiful pearl and maroon Revmaster Offy owned and driven by Don Horvath.

Curly Wetteroth and Emil Deidt created the beautiful blue and silver #5 Speed Age Special, owned by Duane Carter.

Grilles

Grilles are not likely to have survived the rigors of a 20 - 30 year racing career because they were delicate and they were the recipient of heavy impact in crashes.

There are exceptions to every rule and some distinctive grilles, like the ones on Bruce Homeyer's "Konstant Hot Special" can be traced back to the Ryan Offy.

The Snook Offy was another car with a distinctive grille that survived.

Radius Rod Pads

Something as insignificant as the pad that secured the radius rods to the chassis cannot be disregarded as a point of identification.

On early 1946 K.K.'s the top of the rear radius rod pad was even with the bottom of the cockpit side panel on the first thirty cars produced by Kurtis.

At some point after the 30th car but before the 41st car, the pad location was raised an inch requiring a notch in the cockpit side panel (see photo of the Gdula Offy, top of page, note rear radius rod pad is even with the side panel).

Radius Rods/Side Bumpers

Radius rods and side bumpers took a lot of abuse and are rarely found intact with the car.

Some radius rods were very distinctive. Some had vertical pieces of tubing welded between the hairpin.

Charlie Pritchard reinforced the front radius rods of the Tuffanelli Offies with steel plates (see chassis #91 & #92) (pages 55 & 56).

Quarter Elliptical Springs

The quarter elliptical spring setup was half a transverse spring secured to an "L" shaped box, welded to the frame.

The spring was held in place by shackle bolts. The eye of the spring was fastened to the front axle by a bracket on the axle.

An interesting quarter elliptical setup was found on the Marv Edwards car. The car was equipped with quarter elliptical springs on all four corners. Edwards made the setup work by removing and re-arching the springs every week! Marv owned "Hollywood Spring and Axle" and could afford to do this on a weekly basis, an impracticality for the average racer.

Quarter elliptical springs were found on perhaps a dozen of the first cars. I actually documented eleven cars with this setup. I don't believe any original quarter elliptical setups exist today.

The design was so flawed that owners quickly modified their cars to accept transverse springs or torsion bars.

If you have a car that you feel might be one of the very early cars, the frame should bear marks from the grinding employed to remove the welds.

Torsion/Transverse Spring

It is a simple matter to document the suspension that a car had.

Sometimes this is a reliable method of determining if the car you own and the target car match up, using old photos or the memory of the former owner, drivers or pit members.

Remember, some cars were changed from spring to torsion suspension. As newer suspension concepts came into play, they were adapted to the older K.K. chassis.

It is not uncommon to find a K.K. with a cross torsion kit that had been added.

A keen eye can usually spot the welding marks where the spring was mounted on the rear of the frame.

The photo above of Frankie Cavanaugh in the #103 Magarian V8-60 clearly illustrates the quarter elliptical spring setup.

Paint

With rare exceptions the paint on the car you bought will hardly resemble the paint that was on the car in the heyday of the midget boom.

If you received the old belly pans and side panels, check to see if they have multi layers of paint.

The belly pans on a car were not treated with the same care that the hood, nose and tail were.

The owner would scuff the previous layer of paint and shoot another layer over the top.

A technique that can be employed on such panels is a feathering technique.

Starting with a dime sized spot, where you have removed all the paint down to the aluminum, sand an elliptical pattern into the surface. This will reveal the layers of colors like the rings in a tree.

The next step is to get in touch with someone who knows the car and ask them what colors were applied in what order.

The correspondent might say that the car was black, red, cream, blue, orange, yellow, etc. If the colors revealed by your sanding are in the same order it is one more point of identification.

Use common sense. If one of the colors is inconsistent with what you have found, don't assume that you are incorrect. Your correspondents memory may be suspect. Check photos.

The same method can be used to check colors on the chassis. Even if the chassis has been sandblasted and repainted you may still find remnants of color behind the steering bracket, around the seat bracket, under the radius rod pads or around the fuel tank.

Replica or Restoration

The last item to be addressed is a bit more general, rather than specific.

There is some confusion about what constitutes an authentic restoration.

Most restorers and historians would agree that the car must contain a *major portion* of the original chassis.

More collectors and restorers would agree that the construction of an entire car around a cowl hoop or a couple of radius rods is not a legitimate restoration.

As a general rule, let logic be your guide. The chassis is the skeleton of the car to which body panels and running gear were attached. It was the chassis that carried the driver. Therefore the chassis is the car.

The former #12 Bourgnon Offy, restored by Jim Barclay, is a car that had the original chassis replaced. A beautiful car, but is it a restoration or a replica?

Chapter Twelve

The Men Behind the Wheel

While the facts and figures regarding the ownership of Kurtis - Kraft midgets is important, this book would be incomplete if I omitted a chapter dedicated to the men who etched their names in the annals of racing history behind the wheel of the venerable K.K. midget.

The sight of a K.K. midget being twisted to the limit still lingers in the memories of everyone privileged to have witnessed the great midget duels of the 40s, 50s and 60s.

The names of the drivers who fueled our youthful imaginations with lasting, vivid images will never be forgotten!

In the hands of skilled and daring men, the little Kurtis workhorse won thousands of main events in the twenty-five years that it held center stage at speedways all over the United States!

To illustrate how dominate the Kurtis - Kraft midget was in the post war period from 1946 to 1949 I assembled a list of 23 drivers who accounted for over 1,000 main event wins in K.K. midgets!

A.R.D.C.

"Bronco" Bill Schindler was Frank Kurtis' best salesman. This affable, one legged legend, from Freeport, New York, wheeled Mike Caruso's famous two car team to 53 main event wins in 1947, backed up with another 53 wins in 1948.

1947 A.R.D.C. Champ, Georgie Rice won 39 main events in 1947.

Dapper Ted Tappett pulled down 28 wins in 1947 and followed it up with 40 wins in 1948 driving for Frank Curtis.

Mike Nazaruk, the feisty ex-Marine from Bellmore, New York, put Buck Wheeler and Mike Caruso's cars in the winner circle 19 times in 1948.

The unheralded, Steve McGrath matched Nazaruk's record with 19 main event wins in the Lucarelli and Jolson - Edwards Offies in 1948.

Top: Bill Schindler in the Caruso Offy at West Haven, Connecticut.

Bottom: Ted Tappett in the Cheesman Offy.

U.C.O.A./B.S.M.R.A.

In the Northeast, Lowell, Massachusetts', **Johnny Thomson** annexed 32 victories in 1948 driving the Jack Rose and MacLeod Offies.

Joe Sostillio pulled down a remarkable 48 main event wins driving his own Leader Card Offy in 1948.

R.M.M.R.A.

The wunderkind of Rocky Mountain Midget Racing was ex-Marine **Johnnie Tolan** who managed 47 wins in 1947 and 27 more in 1948.

Top Left: Mike Nazaruk in the Mike Caruso #3.

Bottom Left: Georgie Rice in his favorite car - the Eddie Bourgnon Offy.

Top Right: The quiet man, Johnny Thomson, let his driving do the talking for him. Williams Grove 1954.

Bottom Right: Joe Sostillio was an outstanding driver in the Northeast. Williams Grove 1954.

U.R.A.

On the West Coast, **Allen Heath**, dubbed the Seattle Screwball, was making history in Tom Carsten's car. Heath ran it in the Pacific Northwest and with U.R.A. in Southern California. In 1946 Heath notched 31 victories. In 1947 he won an even 50!

Billy Cantrell distinguished himself in U.R.A. Red Circuit competition in 1948 with 33 trips to the winners circle.

Johnny Mantz excelled in the U.R.A. Red Circuit ranks, putting together 28 wins in 1947 while driving the Kittinger Redding V8-60.

Perry Grimm visited the winners circle 22 times in 1947 in Vic Edelbrock's hot two car team, consisting of the famous "Offy Killer" V8-60 and Offy sister car.

Monopoly **Mack Hellings** was cleaning up on the other side of the street in U.R.A.'s Blue Circuit. In 1947 the dapper driver put the A.J. Walker Offy in the win column 29 times.

B.C.R.A.

In Northern California's B.C.R.A. ranks, **Freddie Agabashian** was showing the boys the short way around in George Bignotti's hot V8-60. In 1947 Freddie notched 27 main event wins. In 1948 he won 28 features and added 12 more to his record in 1949.

Jerry Piper fell slightly short of Freddie's tally with 25 main events in 1948.

Fred Friday won 18 mains in 1947 and 11 in 1948.

Top: Johnny Tolan at Soldier Field 1948.

Center: Allen Heath in the #4 at Balboa 1949.

Bottom: Bill Cantrell at Balboa 1949.

216

Top Left: Johnny Mantz at San Berdoo'.

Center Left: Mack Hellings shows off some hardware!

Top Right: Jerry Piper in Rudy Hennig's car.

Center Right: Fred Friday in his own car in 1948.

Lower Right: Freddie Agabashian in Ike Baumbach's car.

MICHIGAN/OHIO VALLEY

The Ohio Valley and Great Lakes area became the stomping grounds of the "Missouri Madman", **Ralph Pratt**, wheeling the Lutes/Gdula and Jim White Offies to 32 wins in 1947, 48 wins in 1948 and 35 more mains in 1949.

In 1947 and 1948 West Coast transplant, **Eddie Johnson** won over 35 main events in the Michigan - Ohio Valley area.

A.A.A.

Henry Banks toured the country with the Lindsey Hopkins Offy midget, winning 30 races in 1947.

In 1948 two time Indy 500 winner, **Bill Vukovich** repeated Banks feat annexing 30 races in the Gerhardt Offy.

IOWA

Danny Kladis showed the folks in Iowa how potent a K.K. was when he won 57 mains in 1948 driving the famous Eric Lund Offy.

Top Left: Ralph Pratt in the brand new, Ronnie Householder Offy November 1946.

Bottom Left: Eddie Johnson in the Pollock Offy, a famous car in the Ohio area.

Top Right: Henry Banks in Lindsey Hopkins' car at Lakeside Speedway in Denver 1947.

MIDWEST

Midwestern sensation **Chuck Marshall** scored 36 main event wins in the Kansas City midget wars in 1948.

Hoosier, **Gene Force** hit his stride in the 1948 season, notching 27 main event markers.

Top Left: Bill Vukovich in his familiar Gerhardt Offy.

Center Left: Gene Force in the Hively Offy in 1951.

Lower Left: Chuck Marshall in the Bayer - Anderson Offy in 1951.

Top Right: Danny Kladis in the Eric Lund Offy at Soldier Field.

Top: Steve McGrath in the Jolson Offy at Freeport Stadium in 1947.

Bottom: Pierce "Perry" Grimm in Vic Edelbrock's V8-60 at Balboa in 1949.

Conclusion

The market for Kurtis - Kraft race cars and memorabilia is strong. An average midget with an Offy engine is worth approximately $25,000.

The value of these cars is almost certain to appreciate if people treat these cars with the same attention to detail and historical accuracy that is lavished on vintage passenger cars.

I have been contacted by a number of people who begin the conversation by saying, "I just bought chassis 143. What can you tell me about it?"

My response is, "What can you tell me about it"?

The process starts by tracing the car as far back as the buyer can until you find someone who was connected with the car when it was raced.

If your car went through the hands of three or four people who merely purchased the car as a restoration project, it is unlikely these people will be able to shed light on the cars racing history.

When you locate a person who owned or drove the car you purchased, get every bit of information you can no matter how contradictory or inconsequential it may seem!

Find out the names of previous owners and drivers. Find out what kind of engine(s) was employed. Learn the name of sponsors, colors and numbers the car carried.

Even if you manage to contact the last owner of the car long after its glory days, that person can begin your journey back through time to the original owner.

Remember a K.K. Midget without a history is far less valuable than a car with a known history.

I hope this volume serves to preserve the history and enhance the value of America's greatest race car — the Kurtis - Kraft midget.

INDEX   Bold type = photo